To CHRISTINE WITH LOVE AND FROM [signature]

JUST DOUGLAS

A NAVIGATOR'S STORY

By
James Douglas Hudson DFC AE RAFVR

[signature] Douglas Hudson
DFC AE RAFVR
30-07-2010

First Published in Great Britain in 2010 by TUCANN *Books*
Text & Images © James Douglas Hudson
All rights reserved
Design © TUCANN*design&print*

ISBN 978-1-907516-03-0

Produced by: TUCANN*design&print*, 19 High Street, Heighington Lincoln LN4 1RG
Tel & Fax: 01522 790009 • www.tucann.co.uk

I dedicate this book to my late wife, parents and Edna Chapman my bomb-aimer's widow.

Their undemonstrative bravery, throughout times of great anxieties, epitomizes that of thousands of other brave people who made similar sacrifices. There were no medals for them in recognition of their stoical, silent service to their countries.

Future generations dwell on this. Strike for them medals of remembrance and thank them all for contributing to a great deliverance.

This book is also my tribute to prisoners of war in Vichy French North Africa who were incarcerated between August 1940 and November 1942.

My stories that follow refer to experiences of British and Allied servicemen from all over the world confined in Vichy French North African prisoner of war camps during this period.

I also was a prisoner in three of these camps for two and a quarter years. In consequence the stories I relate are based on first hand experiences. The descriptions are often explicit and may come as a surprise to many readers.

POLARIS THE POLE STAR

THE CELESTIAL COMPASS, SHEPHERD
AND NAVIGATOR'S FRIEND.

One of a myriad heavenly bodies ever present in the canopy of a star embroidered Firmamental Tapestry, the North Star provides and sustains hope and eternal latitude for the beleaguered traveller. At the rising of the sun this Shepherd in Ursa Minor abandons the Celestial Compass to return by nightfall.

Follow the Plough, continue past Capella to Aldebaran and seek the Pleiades, named the Seven Sisters worshipped throughout history by ancient civilisations.

From the Square of Pegasus find the Chair of Cassiopeia and rest, then join the Hunter in the belt of brilliant Orion.

Ride the Winged Horse Pegasus into battle with Perseus supported by Sagittarius the Archer.

During this firmamental journey the reliable Polaris Celestial Compass, unmoved, required no correction.

CREATION

It is comprehensible to many navigators and some lay people that a great circle is a circle on the surface of a sphere, the plane of which passes through the centre of the sphere and thus divides it into two equal parts.

What follows is the author's understanding of what is not comprehensible to most people.

In the beginning, by the hand of Almighty God, a celestial great circle was born of such magnitude it embraced the firmament and eternity. Creation had arrived, destined to travel within this celestial environment for evermore.

Preordination, or call it fate, decreed that all creation of today's generations travel the same path as travelled by their forbears. Descendent generations will travel an identical pattern.

World without end

PREFACE

This book is of particular importance to those who wish to be both informed of and inspired by the real life stories of this remarkable 93 year old gentleman and ex RAF navigator, Mr James Douglas Hudson.

As revealed by this new book, Douglas remains generous with his time and his exceptional literary skills have ensured that enthusiastic readers may be enlightened to the difficulties of wartime experience, to his own service as a navigator in the RAF, to the dreadful conditions of his time spent as a prisoner of war and especially more recently as an ambassador for those of Bomber Command who sadly lost their lives during 1939 to 1945.

The narrative is of an easy but engaging style. Douglas is an excellent communicator as is clearly demonstrated throughout the book. His autobiography is educational for the younger readers. It is equally appealing to those who have themselves served in the RAF, both old and young, and those who have connections with the Bomber Command squadrons. The narrative is supplemented by important wartime photographs.

His style of writing mirrors the manner in which he would speak to his various audiences. On reading the book you are listening to him as he would speak in day to day conversation or when he is asked to speak publicly about his life in the RAF and of Bomber Command. He describes the events of his own life, of wartime events and of the emotional challenges of health, welfare and relationships of his crew. The conditions of prisoner of war camps are graphically described. He recalls typical scenarios on board the aircraft, many technical facts and figures, and details genuine personal and operational records.

This autobiography is about his personal and professional achievements as an RAF navigator. It describes Douglas' lifetime achievements, his current efforts and activities that relate to developing and maintaining the public interest in the historic events so wonderfully recorded in this book. The book describes how he has relatively recently formed excellent associations with various groups ranging from local colleges, the ATC, The Lincolnshire Aviation Heritage Centre, The Lincolnshire's Lancaster Association Ltd, and Battle of Britain Memorial Flight. He is referenced in various media archives. This autobiography is a resource that is precious to us as it describes in detail his survival. He is one of only a few of his generation still alive. These memories are invaluable to society.

Sandra Morton MSc, MBA, FIBMS, CSi.

PREFACE

There are those who did not come back, who left a void in our eternal consciousness such were the brave men and women of Bomber Command during 1939-1945. For some WW2 is a distant memory, for others it is the conflict which thankfully ended the Nazi expansion across a beaten and humiliated Europe. It is hard to imagine what our lives would be like today if this small island had fallen, we paid a high price during those dark years. No one knows that better than Douglas Hudson DFC AE RAFVR. Here is a man in his ninety fourth year (at time of writing) who tirelessly campaigns for the recognition of all who served in Bomber Command. His writings are a first-hand account, captured in a time capsule of peak experience, he is our living link to all those faded faces and voices we no longer hear. Douglas remembers the young airmen, the look of trepidation as they climbed into their aircraft, knowing as he did; each and every time they flew they might not come back.

I commend this outstanding and gifted book to you, in the surety that in it you will find a rich resonating voice calling out to you to remember.

Marguerite Rami
2009

PREFACE

In the year 2009, seventy years after the beginning of World War 2, fate destined that I should meet James Douglas Hudson. It was at East Kirkby Aviation Centre where I had been engaged to sing. Douglas was signing copies of his latest book. We hit it off immediately. Anybody who is fortunate enough to know Douglas will know exactly what I mean when I say that he is a wonderfully spirited and engaging man. Within no time at all he was up on the stage with me! I sang, we danced together and he spoke of his wartime experiences with gallantry and respect. We soon had our own double act! This is a typical example of 'Just Douglas'. Since then, I have the honour and privilege of calling him my friend. He has my deepest admiration.

On reading one of Douglas' books, you are not only learning about the history of World War 2, you are experiencing everything through the feelings and thoughts of somebody who was actually there. Someone who lived through the hell of being held prisoner and then carried on to take part in many death defying flights as part of Bomber Command. All of this is told in a compelling, moving and personal way. Douglas talks about his life before the War and the wonderful times that were to follow when he arrived home safe and sound. He also never fails to remind us of the many thousands of men and women who didn't. Douglas has so much respect and admiration for his fellow men in Bomber Command and he constantly endeavours to keep their memory in our hearts. Douglas' work is an invaluable source of history chronicled for future generations to read and digest.

When Douglas called me one evening to ask me to write a Preface for this book, I was moved to tears. When he said it was to be called 'Just Douglas' I had to smile! To me he is so much more than 'Just Douglas'. He is an Ambassador, a Public Figure, an Historian, an Author, a Father, a Friend, an Inspiration and, above all, a Hero.

Lola Lamour (Joanne Massey)

Introducing Myself
AUTOBIOGRAPHICAL RECOLLECTIONS

World War One, known as The Great War, was allegedly fought to end all wars. That was the mistaken belief of the pundits and most ordinary citizens. In reality it served to engender World War Two. From 3rd of August 1914 when Germany invaded Belgium, battles raged until 11th November 1918 at which date the Armistice, signed by the Germans, proclaimed an end to hostilities. I mention a few famous and horrific battles, namely Mons, Ypres, The Somme, Passchendale and Arras, in which hundreds of thousands of brave soldiers gave their lives for their countries. They fought in appalling conditions of stench and detritus to gain a few yards of territory, very often to be retaken quickly by the enemy.

In no man's land shells whistled overhead and burst on the ground creating thunderous flaming explosions. Men's limbs and

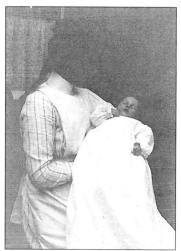

bodies were flung everywhere, many back into the trenches earlier vacated before going over the top for the offensive.

On 21st May 1916 at Whitkirk near Leeds, it was as though nature's electric discharge, a vivid flash of lightning followed by an almost unprecedented crash of thunder, precipitated the birth of a baby boy, to Phyllis Hudson née Pilley, wife of Harold Ernest Hudson.

Douglas and Nurse Palmer, 1916

The baby was christened James Douglas, generally to be known as Douglas. I was that baby.

On 11th November 1918, at the age of two and a half years, I can still remember clearly seeing a large Union Jack Flag flying from the bedroom window of the house next door in Carter Avenue. At that age I did not of course understand its significance.

My parents moved to Whitley Bay near Newcastle in 1919. It was near there at Felling I was taken to Santa Claus's workshop where he showed me a lovely blue toy motor car. I asked if he would please bring it to me for Christmas. HE DID and brightened the day for a delighted little boy. From then, until the age of nine, I was a firm believer in Santa Claus. The joy of Santa Claus should be the privilege and encouraged belief for all children.

Father entered into partnership with a colleague and they opened a laundry at Felling. Sadly the business failed. An honest man of high principles, Father paid all his creditors in full out of income he received as textiles dyeworks' manager with a firm at Cornholme in the Todmorden/Burnley valley. In those days the valley was damp, sooty and smoke laden from mill chimneys and the rows upon rows of back to back houses.

I was a frail child and suffered from what was described as constitutional weakness with rheumatoid tendencies. The family doctor told my parents that they would not rear me unless we moved from the valley. I was often away from school, which I did not attend until the age of six and a half and spent much time in bed for enforced rest. From my bedroom window I could watch the children play in the school yard. Before starting school I could not recite the alphabet, yet one year later, believe it or not, I was the best reader in the infants' class. When not poorly, I led an active life running wild, roaming and climbing the moors. We stayed in the valley a further five years from 1922 to 1927 before moving to Skipton in Yorkshire.

Cornholme Board School 1924 includes (a) Bessie Whiteside, (b) Clifford Hodgeson, (c) Charlie Holden, our teacher (Alice M Law, and (e) myself

Hilton Leader Ingfield Terrace with Airdale dog, Bess and myself 1926

Myself and friends at Vale, 1926

At Cornholme, two young men Arthur and Harry who worked in the dyeworks laboratory for Father, and who enjoyed Mother's regular catering hospitality, bought a huge box of fireworks to the value of one pound, before each 5ᵗʰ November. That was a lot of money in those days, but gave great pleasure to me and many neighbours' children.

Mother and father

Harry told me intriguing stories about The Great War and read from the Bystander Magazine by Bruce Bairnsfather, who depicted with clever illustrations, two cockney soldier characters Bill and Bert.

A cartoon I remember showed the pair obviously trying to delouse, sitting in a shell-hole full of filthy water up to their chins. Under the eye of a Belgian peasant woman holding the hand of a child, the expression on their faces said it all. The caption read, "Tell er to op it Bert, I'm sittin' on a bit of shell or somethink." Another depicted a raven perched on the top of a tall chimney pot, under which a large hole had been made in the chimney breast by a passing German shell that continued unexploded on its way. The simple caption read, ""Duds," quoth the raven!" I didn't know what that meant.

Bairnsfather had his own inimitable style of depicting the dreadful detritus of no man's land. The following remain clear to me. The first of a brilliant moonlit night in England and a young lady gazing towards the sky from her bedroom open window, saying, "To think it is the same dear old moon shining down on him." The second showed him in no man's land somewhere in Belgium, under the same moon, up to his ankles in mud, repairing barbed wire defences. Shells were shrieking overhead, there were explosions all over the sky and Very-lights illuminating bodies. Caption "This blinkin' moon will be the death of us."

I started to read Bystanders before I was eight and at the same time received my first annual called the Oojah Annual, from which I remember three simple verses:-

"Good natured Godfrey gives to his chums,
all his cakes and keeps only the crumbs.
Painstaking Pansy is doing her best,
to teach every cuckoo to build its own nest.
Terrible Thomas with sword and with gun,
looks just as fierce as a regular Hun."

We became friendly with a Mr and Mrs Penny who enjoyed early retirement supported by the proceeds from the sale of a profitable fish and chip business. Chips were almost a staple diet for the impoverished out of work mill workers. One pennyworth of chips daily was all most could afford. A fish in batter at twopence (2d) was normally beyond their budget.

Mrs Penny was a small agile, nimble lady who dressed in black and wore black lace-up boots. She often accompanied me scrambling on the moors and once showed me a skylark's nest well camouflaged in the heather. I was not allowed to touch a single egg.

I loved what Mr Penny called our 'bachelor tea' on Saturday afternoons. We sat at a bare wooden table, scrubbed spotlessly clean, enjoyed a superb meat and potato pie served on willow pattern plates, and drank tea from a pint mug.

Another treat was to accompany Bert Jowett on the dyeworks' light lorry, a converted thirty horsepower Buick limousine, to deliver dyed yarns to the Yorkshire mills. Bert provided food wrapped in newspaper for lunch, as was the tea, a mixture of tea leaves in thick condensed milk. This concoction was mashed in boiling water, almost steam, from an outside tap in the mill yard. From whence it came I know not. The resultant drink, in a pint mug of course, was super and I never suffered unpleasant after effects.

My friend Hilton was older than the other boys and was also my carer. No harm would come to me with Hilton around. He ran a newspaper round and came from a large family of thirteen. Often he would have gone without a meal had Mother not provided one for him.

In January 1927 I was sorry to leave the valley where, in spite of unemployment and hardship, people were very kind. Whenever possible, Mothers would bake their renowned meat and potato pies. Children would play in the streets clutching huge homemade helpings containing more potato than meat. I had confounded medical opinion and survived more than five years in that damp and smoky valley.

Now I was to enter life at Skipton, where Father had taken a new managerial job. I was to be sent to Ermysted's Grammar School, where fools and the idle were not suffered gladly. The school was founded in 1492 by Peter Toller, re-founded in 1548 by William Ermysted and in 1719 Sylvester Petyt became benefactor. It has been described as a school of great antiquity, the endowment of the Foundation being mainly applied towards the reduction of fees, which in 1927 were £9 16s 6d a year including the cost of books. Boarding fees were an additional £63.

As the only new boy to arrive in early Lent term 1927, I was an easy candidate for bullying. Fortunately the new boy novelty soon wore off; I became accepted and settled down unmolested to a normal, albeit tough school life. Ermysted's did not tolerate the faint hearted.

The concept was that strenuous physical exercise induced greater capacity for mental study. This required attendance at school on Saturday mornings. Tuesday and Thursday afternoons in autumn and Lent terms were reserved for playing Rugby, cross country running and athletics. Summer term activities were swimming and cricket. For the latter we had the benefit of an excellent large flat turfed ground called 'The Top' equipped with a pavilion. It has been described in a prospectus as, 'a large first-class ground, as fine as any school in the north of England.'

At morning prayers in Big School, the Head Master would call all Roman Catholics to fall out.

I was impressed by the cars, many of which were cabriolets, parked in the High Street by the cattle market. There was the Trojan, a vehicle that had solid tyres. Others included the Bull Nose Morris Oxford and Morris Cowley, Austin, Wolseley, Riley, Clyno, Singer, The Model T Ford, Citroën, Renault, Chevrolet, Buick, Chrysler, Dèlage, Donnet, Packard and Daimler. Their owners would be professional businessmen, local mill owners and wealthy farmers from the dales.

Bullying had made me resolute to stand adversity. I enjoyed participation and whilst never an outright winner, played in the colts fifteen Rugby set during my last year at Ermysted's.

When Father moved to another position in the Manchester area I stayed at Ermysted's for one year as a boarder in School House. I disliked the lack of privacy of communal living and was fortunate in passing the entrance exam to The Manchester Grammar School in July 1930.

The Manchester Grammar School (MGS) was founded in 1515 by Hugh Oldham, Bishop of Exeter. At the 1931 Founder's Day Service held in Manchester Cathedral, we learned he was motivated by Mancunian boys being pregnant with wit. This Service was prior to the opening of the new school buildings at Fallowfield south of the city, when it was stated, "The owl has opened its wings and flown to a fairer greener place."

I joined the school in September 1930 at Long Millgate in the city, before the owl had opened its wings. There would be 1250 to 1300 boys, more than four times the number at Ermysted's, where I knew them all. I found it impersonal and again although I started as the only new boy to the school in my class, I was not bullied. Classes were divided into modern, classical and science with separate maths forms, which would accommodate boys from any of these groups. They were all streamed. The modern group was streamed from A to E and I was in the B stream,

Father bowler hat and rolled up umbrella and myself, Ilkley Tarn 1928

(Below) Skipton schoolhouse Ermysted Boys 1930 - Including front row: Myself, Scott, Tyson, Rigby (Killed WW2) Back row: George Hully (Killed Spanish Civil War), Thwaite, Arnold Blezzard

19

(Above) School House, Ermysted's Grammar School, Skipton, 1930. Douglas front row fourth from left.

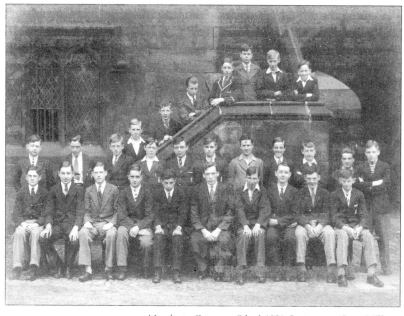

Manchester Grammar School, 1931. Last year at Long Millgate Douglas: top of steps second from right. Form Master Mr J.P. Bowden MA.

September 1931 First Day of arrival at new school

Manchester Grammar School, 1932, first year at new school Fallowfield. Douglas standing far right. Form Master Mr J.P. Bowden MA.

21

which I found quite difficult. Those in the A stream were relative geniuses. At morning prayers in Main Assembly Hall, the High Master would call Roman Catholics and Jews to fall out.

After leaving school I applied regularly for jobs advertised in The Manchester Guardian, as it was called then, under the section Boys, Youths and Apprentices. It was four months before I received a reply. After my first success I never failed in future applications.

To get away from the smog of Manchester I enjoyed cycling holidays to the Lake District and even the West Country. I was fascinated watching cars fail in their drivers' attempts to climb Porlock, Countisbury and Lynton hills. I then graduated to motorbikes and from 1936 to the outbreak of WW2 enjoyed extensive tours, particularly in the Scottish Highlands. Rannoch Moor at sunset in August 1938 will remain in my memory for all time.

Earning a living in Manchester was not a glamorous occupation. I could not afford to embark on a short service commission as a pilot in the Royal Air Force. Young officers, unsupported financially, had difficulty living on their pay. Father was undergoing a period of impoverishment in the depressed textiles' trade. There was a waiting list of over a year for training as a pilot in the Manchester Volunteer Reserve, so in June 1939 I joined as an air observer, later to be known as navigator.

After a brief holiday in which I took Mother as pillion passenger on my motorbike touring the West Country, we returned to Manchester shortly before Neville Chamberlain announced to the country that we were at war with Germany.

I was called up immediately and entered into flying training at Prestwick No. 1 Air Observer Navigation School early in November 1939. Here members of the Manchester Volunteer Reserve joined members from the Belfast and West Hartlepool Volunteer Reserves. We flew from a huge grass airfield and carried out our navigational training in two ex Dutch Airlines'

Fokker aircraft and the most reliable Avro Anson.

Bombing and gunnery training followed at Evanton, Cromarty Firth, where we flew in the Handley Page Harrow, Fairey Battle, Avro Anson and the open cockpit Westland Wallace.

My training continued at Bicester, where I flew in the then famous fighter bomber aircraft, namely the Marks 1 and 4 Bristol Blenheims. This was my last training before posting to 101 Blenheim Squadron at RAF West Raynham in Norfolk.

I arrived at West Raynham on 4th July 1940 to join 101 Blenheim Squadron, an airfield we shared with 18 Blenheim Squadron. It was here I met my pilot D. C .B. 'John' Riddick and wireless operator-air gunner D. W. G. 'Tony' Randall. Most raids were infiltration seeking occupied airfields, particularly since the fall of Dunkirk, and barge concentrations in anticipation of the Nazis invading the UK. Bomber Command was not yet strong enough to take the war to the enemy.

During the seven weeks we were at West Raynham the Station lost 20 Blenheims.

After Prime Minister Neville Chamberlain announced in September 1939 we were at war with Germany, a period followed which had been referred to as the phoney war. This had now changed and we were to enter the period known as The Battle of Britain during the latter period of 1940.

I quote two damning examples concerning 82 Squadron based at Watton:

17th May 1940. Twelve Blenheims were ordered to attack Gembloux in Belgium to harass the Nazi invading army. All twelve were lost.

12th August 1940. The same squadron received orders for twelve Blenheims to attack Aalborg in Denmark. Eleven aircraft failed to return.

AIR PUBLICATION 1234
(*Revised April*, 1935)
(*Reprinted April*. 1938)

DEFINITIONS

1. *Air navigation* is the art of conducting an aircraft from place to place by dead reckoning and fixing position by observations of terrestrial objects and celestial bodies. It includes the ability to maintain a given direction in or above clouds and mist, and by night.

2. *Air speed* is the speed of an aircraft relative to the air.

3. *Axis of the Earth* is that diameter about which it revolves.

4. *Azimuth.—See " Bearing ".*

5. *Bearing.*—(i) The *great circle bearing* of an object is the angle at the observer between the meridian passing through the observer and the great circle joining his position to the object. This may also be called the *azimuth*. The angle is measured clockwise from the meridian from 0° to 360°. (Fig. 1.)

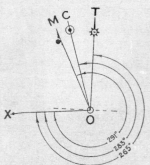

Fig. 1.—True Bearing = Angle T.O.X. = 265°.
Magnetic Bearing = Angle M.O.X. = 291°.
Compass Bearing = Angle C.O.X. = 283".
Variation = Angle T.O.M. = 26° W.
Deviation = Angle M.O.C. = 8° E.
Compass Error = Angle T.O.C. = 18° W.

(ii) Bearings are called *true* or *magnetic*, according to whether the angles are measured from the true meridian or the magnetic meridian.

(iii) In a *compass bearing* the angle is measured from the direction of a particular compass needle.

(iv) Bearings may be referred to the course of an aircraft, and are then measured from ahead through 180° to port and starboard, being termed respectively *red* and *green*. In Fig. 2 the bearing of A is Green 45°, and of B Red 120°.

(v) The *mercatorial bearing* is the angle at the observer between his meridian and a rhumb line joining him to the object.

6. *Cardinal points.*—The directions north, east, south and west. (Usually written N., E., S., W.)

7. *Compass error* is the algebraic sum of variation and deviation. (Figs. 1 and 3.)

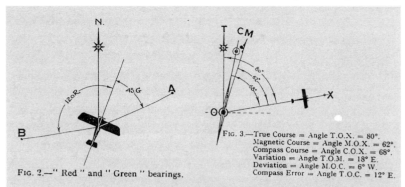

FIG. 2.—" Red " and " Green " bearings.

FIG. 3.—True Course = Angle T.O.X. = 80°.
Magnetic Course = Angle M.O.X. = 62°.
Compass Course = Angle C.O.X. = 68°.
Variation = Angle T.O.M. = 18° E.
Deviation = Angle M.O.C. = 6° W.
Compass Error = Angle T.O.C. = 12° E.

8. *Contour.*—The representation on a map of an imaginary line running along the surface of the ground at the same height above sea level throughout its length. A *form line* is an approximate contour.

9. *Conversion angle.*—The angle between the great circle and mercatorial bearings. (Fig. 4.)

10. *Couple.*—When two equal forces act on a body in opposite directions, they constitute a *couple.* The couple is the product of one of the forces and the perpendicular distance between them.

11. *Course.*—(i) The *true course* is the angle between the longitudinal axis of an aircraft and the true meridian. (Fig. 3.)

(ii) The *magnetic course* is the angle between the longitudinal axis of an aircraft and the magnetic meridian.

(iii) The *compass course* is the angle between the longitudinal axis of an aircraft and the direction of a particular compass needle.

12. *Dead reckoning* consists of calculating the track and ground speed of an aircraft. The *D.R. position* is the position arrived at by dead reckoning.

13. *Deviation* is the angle, measured in the horizontal plane, between the magnetic meridian and the direction of a particular compass needle influenced by a magnetic field not coincident with the earth's magnetic field. It is named E. (+) or W. (−), according to whether the north-seeking pole lies to the east or west of the magnetic meridian. (Figs. 1 and 3.)

14. *Dip* of a magnetic needle is the angle in the vertical plane between the horizontal and the direction of the earth's line of total magnetic force. Sometimes called *magnetic inclination.*

15. *Drift* is the angle between the longitudinal axis of an aircraft and the track : it is measured to port or starboard relative to the aircraft's head.

16. *Equator* of the Earth is the great circle of which the plane is at right angles to the axis. (W.E. in Fig. 4.)

17. *Fix.*—The position of an aircraft as determined on a map or chart, generally by the intersection of two or more position lines.

18. *Force.*—Any cause which tends to alter a body's state of rest or uniform motion in a straight line.

19. *Gradient.*—A rate of rise or fall, often expressed as a fraction. Thus 1/30 represents a rise or fall of 1 unit vertically in 30 units horizontally.

20. *Graticule.*—The network formed on a map by meridians and parallels of latitude.

21. *Grid.*—The representation on a map of a rectangular co-ordinate system.

22. *Great circle* is a circle on the surface of a sphere, the plane of which passes through the centre of the sphere and thus divides it into two equal parts. The shortest distance between any two points on the surface of a sphere is the arc of a great circle joining the points. (*See* Fig. 4.)

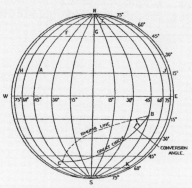

Fig. 4.—The Earth, showing latitude, longitude, great circle and rhumb line, etc.

23. *Ground speed* is the speed of an aircraft relative to the ground.

24. *Hachuring* is a conventional method of representing hill features on a map by shading in short disconnected lines, which are drawn in the direction of the steepest slopes.

25. *Horizontal equivalent.*—The distance in plan between two adjacent contours. (Written H.E.)

26. *Inertia.*—The tendency of a body to resist a change of motion.

27. *Isobar.*—A line drawn on a weather map, at all points on which the atmospheric pressure has the same value.

28. *Isoclinal.*—A line drawn on a map or chart, at all points on which the magnetic dip has the same value.

29. *Isogonal.*—A line drawn on a map or chart, at all points on which the magnetic variation has the same value. The *agonic line* is the line of no variation.

30. *Knot* is a unit of speed : it is a speed of one nautical mile an hour.

31. *Latitude* of a place is the arc of the meridian between the equator and the place and is named N. or S. according to whether the place is north or south of the equator. (In Fig. 4, Lat. of A = 15° N. ; Lat. of K = 60° S.)

A *parallel of latitude* is a small circle parallel to the equator. (HAJ in Fig. 4.)

Difference of latitude between two places is the arc of a meridian intercepted between the parallels of the places (written d. Lat.) ; d. Lat. from A to K = 75° S. (Fig. 4.)

32. *Layer tinting.*—A system of representing relief on maps by colouring the map between adjacent contours in a uniform shade, the shade chosen depending on the height.

33. *Longitude* of a place is the smaller arc of the equator intercepted between the prime meridian and the meridian of the place, and is named E. or W. according to whether the place is east or west of the prime meridian. (In Fig. 4, Long. of A = 45° W. ; Long. of K = 75° E.)

Difference of longitude between two places is the smaller arc of the equator intercepted between the meridians of the places (written d. Long.) ; d. Long. from K to A = 120° W. (Fig. 4.)

34. *Magnetic equator.*—An imaginary line on the surface of the earth joining all points where the earth's line of total magnetic force is horizontal, i.e. where the angle of dip is zero.

35. *Magnetic field.*—The region round a magnet in which its magnetism has effect.

36. *Magnetic meridian.*—The great circle on the earth at any place in the plane of which a magnetic needle would be, if freely suspended and influenced only by the earth's magnetic field.

37. *Magnetic poles* of the earth are the two positions on the earth's surface where the earth's line of total magnetic force is vertical, i.e. where the angle of dip is 90°.

38. *Meridian* is a semi-great circle passing through the poles of the earth (NAS, NKS, etc., in Fig. 4).

39. *Natural scale.*—See " *Representative fraction* ".

40. *Nautical mile* is the average length of a minute of latitude measured on any meridian. Its length is generally taken as 6,080 ft. (Symbol '.)

41. *Orienting* a map is the process of setting it so that the meridians on the map lie North and South.

42. *Poles* of the earth are the extremities of its axis of revolution. (N. and S. in Fig. 4.)

43. *Position error* is the error in the reading given by an air speed indicator due to the positioning of the pressure head.

44. *Position line* is a line obtained from observation of a terrestrial object or a celestial body, at some point on which line it is known that the aircraft must be.

45. *Projection* of a map or chart is any orderly system of representing meridians and parallels and the earth's surface on a plane.

46. *Quadrantal points.*—The directions north-east, south-east, south-west and north-west. (Usually written NE., SE., SW., NW.)

47. *Representative fraction* (written R.F.).—The ratio which the distance between two points on a map bears to the distance between the same two points on the ground. The ratio is always expressed as a fraction, of which the numerator is unity. It may also be called the *natural scale*.

48. *Rhumb line* is that curve on the earth's surface which cuts all the meridians it meets at the same angle. (*See* Fig. 4.)

49. *Run* is the direction and distance over the ground which an aircraft travels between two given instants.

50. *Small circle* is a circle on the surface of the sphere, the plane of which does not pass through the centre of the sphere.

51. *Spot height.*—The record on a map of the exact height above sea level of a particular point.

52. *Synoptic chart.*—See "*Weather map*".

53. *Track* is the angle between a meridian and a line representing the actual path of an aircraft relative to the ground. It is measured from 0° to 360° clockwise from the meridian.

54. *Variation* (sometimes called *declination*) is the angle, measured in the horizontal plane, between the true meridian and the direction of a freely suspended magnetic needle influenced only by the earth's magnetic field. It is named E. (+) or W. (−) according to whether the north-seeking end of the needle lies to the east or west of the true meridian. (*See* Figs. 1 and 3.)

55. *Vector* is a straight line which, in both length and direction, represents a quantity such as a force or velocity.

56. *Velocity.*—The rate of change of position of a body in a given direction. Velocity therefore involves both speed and direction.

57. *Vertical interval.*—The difference in level between two adjacent contours. (Written V.I.)

58. *Weather map.*—An outline map on which are recorded meteorological observations made simultaneously at observing stations over a large area. The weather map is the basis of weather forecasting. (Also known as a *synoptic chart.*)

B Course AONS

Self - at Prestwick N° 1 AONS prior to being issued with uniform - November 1939

During The Battle of Britain, Fighter Command kept the Luftwaffe at bay. This action, together with the presence of ships in the Royal Navy between Scapa Flow and the English Channel, prevented a serious Nazi invasion and occupation of our little island.

Towards the end of August my crew and that of Pilot Officer D. K. Macdonald, were taken off the 101 Squadron strength and received orders each to ferry a Blenheim to Heliopolis via Malta.

EVANTON 1940
Left to Right   Self   Harry Bowers   'Sticky' Leach and Alec Buckley

The journey to Heliopolis would be in two stages. First direct to Malta flying over Marseilles to the coast of North Africa and then continue east. We asked to fly to Malta via Gibraltar, land there to refuel and risk using the notorious short runway. The authorities refused to allow this; they thought it presented a greater hazard than lack of fuel by taking the longer route. In spite of both pilots' strong protestations, the matter was taken out of their hands. We carried out four special fuel consumption test flights later, which proved the pilots to be right. Nevertheless, we were ordered to go when the meteorological conditions were favourable. How did they know in those days what the met conditions would be like in the southern Mediterranean?

So, two ex 101 Squadron Blenheims and their crews, left Thorney Island, the most southerly suitable aerodrome in England, en route direct to Malta, at 00.05 hours on 27th August 1940. They lost sight of each other immediately after take-off.

We were soon intercepted by an ME 109 German fighter. The pilot, confused, no doubt believing we were a captured aircraft after Dunkirk returning from an attack on the UK, 'buzzed' us three times, fortuitously without firing a shot!

Fairey Battle

Handley Page Harrow

Myself and Harry Bowers

Noel Hawthorne
Prestwick colleague killed under training

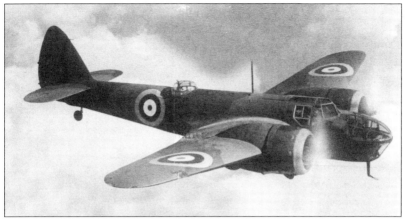

Blenheim

After crossing the French coast near Marseilles I witnessed a magnificent sunrise heralding dawn over the Mediterranean. War did not appear on the horizon! It was exciting with an air almost of mystique as my crew and I continued to the apparently unknown, in reality Egypt, to fly in a desert war.

Later in the flight, well after we had passed the critical point for decision making, everything went wrong. To avoid flying into rapidly increasing cumulonimbus clouds moving towards us from the North African mainland, (clouds which would contain supercooled water droplets that become ice on impact), we had to lose altitude and make a considerable detour. Inevitably we would not reach Malta due to fuel shortage. John, with no alternative, turned the aircraft in the direction of Cap Bon, Tunisia, the nearest landfall, where our Blenheim crash-landed sustaining serious damage to the undercarriage.

The experience of this flight was quite different from any earlier flights. It shaped my immediate destiny and clearly emphasised the unpredictability of weather forecasting. It further manifested the ineptitude of the hierarchy, who had laid on the flights, which resulted in the loss of two Blenheim aeroplanes, had cost three lives and placed three other aircrew in prisoner of war camps for the next two and a quarter years.

It was widely believed in June 1940 after Dunkirk that France's hope of resurgence would lie in North Africa. Her Colonial Empire may prevent France's status sinking to a minor power. Was it on these pretexts the British government based reliance, at the time we were sent to the Middle East, telling us not to destroy our aircraft if we had to land in Vichy French North Africa?

We had become scapegoats in the complex post Dunkirk situation. For almost two and a half years the impotent Vichy French government committed national suicide, whereby France degenerated into a vassal state of the Third Reich to the detriment of the supportive British, the British Empire and Dependencies.

We succeeded in burning our flight documents before being captured and driven under heavy guard in intolerable heat, on narrow, winding, uneven roads through precipitous, arid country, to a fortified military outpost in the hills at Le Kef.

My prisoner of war experience began in a room kept locked overnight. It had heavily barred windows and was housed in a stone built Arabs' barracks confined in this military fortress. There was no help from The American Consul in Tunis. The Vichy French had no conception of hygiene. Sanitary facilities comprised a zinc bath, emptied daily. Our fly infested food, referred to as 'la soupe', consisted of macaroni and sloppy, dirty vegetables, as provided to the Arab soldiers. Disillusionment and imprisonment had begun.

In early September 1940 I lay on my bed in this evil room recovering from dysentery. I was bruised mentally by sudden enforced idleness and abrupt removal from flying participation in a war, now gaining momentum, loaded against the UK. I thought of my colleagues who trained with me at Prestwick, Evanton and Bicester. I thought also of new colleagues with whom I had become acquainted during my brief sojourn with 101 Squadron at West Raynham. I thought of those who had died so early serving their country, the blossom of those whose youth would never mature to fruition. I reflected with great sadness upon the last moments I had spent with some of my colleagues; brave men with enthusiasm for living, who had not counted the cost of dying, but had been plucked by the great reaper, called 'The Chopman'. I recall one young man in particular, Alec Buckley, who chased me up and down the corridor of a pub in Bicester, laughing as he sprayed me with the contents of a soda syphon. This was only days before he was killed flying operationally in a Blenheim bomber from Lossiemouth, as his crew attempted to take the fight to the Nazis. I thought of Harry Bowers, who always smoked a pipe that he packed very carefully with Balkan Sobranie tobacco. Harry rode the tandem bicycle called 'Bogus' with me at Bicester, but never received his twenty shillings spoils from its sale. I could not dismiss the memory of 'Parky' Parkinson from 101 Squadron, who never made his honeymoon leave. His Blenheim aircraft was shot down without trace off Cherbourg. There were many others, including Norman Giblin DFM aged twenty, who was shot down twice and Pilot Officer W. B. Gingell, who survived two Blenheim ditchings from West Raynham and was later killed in a flying accident.

During this period of reflection, I thought I should go crazy. I felt I should go raving mad. Who was I to be spared? I should have been better off dead, or so I thought. This room in the caserne at Le Kef was the epitome of purgatory, a striking example of hell. I had arrived in Hades. I had become crazy, if only temporarily. I was a prisoner of these bastard Vichy French collaborators, utterly devoid of scruples.

As more aircrew prisoners arrived and the accommodation of one single room became crowded, arguments arose engendering disharmony. To help resolve this problem and to carry out our duties as prisoners of war, fellow aircrew colleague Ted Hart and I decided to attempt an escape in early December 1940. The weather was getting colder and the stench of the room in which we were compelled to spend our time was becoming unbearable.

Let me explain the difference between ESCAPE and EVASION. Many readers will have heard about escapees from German prison of war camps who reached Switzerland, or perhaps

Spain. They were repatriated having been captives in Germany, a belligerent country, from which they had escaped to neutral countries. If they had evaded capture in the first place, any neutral country they reached would have interned them.

French North Africa was as described - French. The official answer is - the French were on our side at the beginning of the war, but France became our enemy when the dishonourable Vichy French regime became subservient to and a partner of the German and Italian axis in North Africa. In consequence we were treated immediately as prisoners of war. That, apart from an age-old Anglophobia, explains the evil treatment we received from our captors.

It was said at the time, however, that the Allies may have been at war with Vichy, but there was no instance stating the French were at war with the Allies. I should be interested to receive the bureaucratic explanation.

The wisdom of a child is tempered by naivety and lack of experience. Is child wisdom a conceptional myth? Is it fallacious? Not until nearing adulthood does the child begin to understand compromise, or have the ability to reason more capably for better or worse; regrettably often the latter. What was a beautiful idea; perhaps a satellite of innocence, on becoming mature of age, can engender malaise to be found in leaders of government, ambassadors, captains of industry, dictators and those who wish to usurp power.

Illustrative examples in 1940 included Mussolini, who with Hitler coerced Vichy Leader Marshal Pétain and followers Darlan, Daladier, Laval and others to unite and collaborate with Nazi Germany.

Dysentery in the caserne was prevalent and often resulted afterwards in bouts of unpleasant flatulence. On one Bridge playing occasion, I suffered one of these bouts and had to leave the table repeatedly in consideration of the other players. It was then Ted passed the classic comment I shall never forget, using words to this effect, "Gosh Doug, a rat must have crawled up your backside and died!" (Substitute gosh and backside with words more specifically expressive.)

Self   Wilbur Wright   Ted Hart

Le Kef February 1941

After the evening meal on Sunday 8th December 1940 in appalling weather conditions with driving snow, Ted and I began our escape. Ted scaled the cabinet wall and gave me a helping hand over the top. Tony Randall who had joined us lost his grip, fell backwards and collided with a cistern. The boom of the impact alerted the guards, and Tony was caught immediately with no means of escape.

The alarm was really sounded. Compounded by the problem of driving snow, chaos ensued in the prison camp. Lights appeared from all directions, inside and outside the caserne. In spite of the snow, soldiers and guards emerged in frenzied panic as we ran up a steep hillside away from the Souk el Arba road. We enjoyed with rewarding satisfaction the consternation our escape had caused our captors. Ten minutes later, completely out of breath, we sought the shelter of a rocky outcrop looking down on to the caserne now fully illuminated. By luck we had got it right. The search, according to the flashing lights, was heading downhill towards the station and railway line to Tunis. There was not a light on the road to Souk el Arba, a small town and our destination some forty-eight kilometres away.

With extreme caution we left our rocky outcrop shelter and made our way diagonally away from the direction of the caserne towards the road. All was quiet in the prison camp where the lights remained switched on. By now our captors would have completed the 'appel' and discovered that Ted and I were the only missing prisoners. The guards were increased until daylight although no further attempts at escape were conceivable. Nevertheless, the Vichy French were playing it safe until morning.

Fortunately, the snow ceased quite suddenly and the night remained dry as we trudged along in quagmire conditions. It was incomprehensible how climatic and terrain situations could change so drastically from being hot and arid on our arrival four months earlier.

The road, almost a track, was deserted, but often we became disturbed by the noise of barking dogs. How sounds travel at night. It was disquieting and we became concerned lest the dogs' barking should raise an alert. Perhaps we had nothing to worry about; nevertheless we carried long sticks in case a dog should attack. Ted explained the importance of holding the stick almost horizontally, grasped tightly with hands and arms as far apart as possible. He said an attacking dog would leap and grab the stick in its mouth and hopefully not the person. Fortunately, the need to carry out this procedure did not arise.

We had covered about half the distance to what we understood would be the Mellégue Bridge and stopped for a short rest. Here, lying on a stone ledge in the shelter of an outcrop of rocks, I immediately fell asleep from sheer weariness. Had it not been for Ted's vigilance and prompt alert reaction in arresting my fall, I could have been hurt. As we had covered only half the distance to Souk El Arba we decided to carry on without further delay.

After walking for several hours, we sighted a large river in the valley some distance away. The road crossed over the river by what appeared to be a suspension bridge. We left the road and then approached the bridge by crossing a huge tract of open, steep sloping, boggy land, effectively, on the hypotenuse of a triangle, of which the road formed the two shorter sides. This reduced the distance but not the time, as conditions under foot were atrocious.

Wearily, we arrived at the unguarded bridge and crossed the river that turned out to be the Mellégue, as it flowed in spate from Algeria into Tunisia. It presented an awesome uninviting sight. I shuddered as we peered down from the bridge and looked into its swirling, dark, fast flowing waters. There is something about water in the dark that frightens me. I have nightmares to this day of crossing that Mellégue Bridge.

We continued on the last leg of our journey by road and now, hampered by an increasing stiffness in our tired limbs, it became unwise to rest. Ted expressed concern that our muscles might become locked and seize completely, so we should continue to exercise them. It required determination and strong will power to keep going for the remaining few kilometres. How we made it, I shall never know. Our shoes had absorbed so much water they had become dead weights. Mine began to crocodile. Repair was impracticable other than tying the soles by wrapping them with several layers of string, which fortunately we carried in case of such emergency. We later disguised this problem by lowering our trousers to cover our footwear.

In a state of complete exhaustion, we reached Souk El Arba at 10 o'clock on the Monday morning wearing French army khaki trousers and to conceal our RAF tunics, khaki greatcoats issued previously by our captors. Their 'gifts', which were not intended for this purpose, kept us warm and acted as a disguise. To our relief we did not attract the slightest attention from the locals who obviously assumed we were French soldiers. With all the aplomb we could muster, we entered a small hotel and ordered two coffees. Those drinks served pleasantly and without hesitation, were absolute delectation and the prelude to our booking board and accommodation for the next three days.

Although my knowledge of the language was passable I could not keep up the pretence of being French and explained to our hosts that Ted and I were American graduates carrying out geological studies in liaison with the American and Vichy authorities. They asked to see our passports in evidence and thankfully accepted my explanation that they were lodged with the American Consul in Tunis for safekeeping. America was not yet involved in the war and we both signed the hotel register under pseudo names and addresses with no further questions being asked.

When our hostess left, after showing us to our twin bedded-room, we locked the door and moved a heavy piece of furniture towards it as a barricade in case of an emergency. We took stock of the surroundings outside our room at the back and noticed that from the bedroom window, we could reach the flat roof of a low ground floor building and from there, drop to the ground.

I shall never forget those most comfortable beds. When our heads touched the pillows we became dead to the world until wakened for dinner at 6.30 pm. Should it have been necessary to attempt an emergency escape through the window, I would have failed miserably and I doubt if Ted could have made it either. Sitting up in bed I could scarcely move, being in the grip of extreme muscular tightness. Following gentle, painstaking, physical persuasion under Ted's practical guidance, (remember he was a PT instructor before re-mustering to aircrew), the muscles were encouraged to slacken a little to enable us to negotiate the stairs, but in my case only just. We entered the dining room very gingerly and with some trepidation.

Would word have got through from Le Kef? Might we be identified as the two British escapees? Happily, none of the diners took the slightest notice when we appeared. Could it all have been in our minds? I doubt it, but how important it had become to behave naturally.

Our charming French hostess never betrayed the slightest sign of suspicion regarding our real identity, although Ted and I firmly believed she doubted our being Americans.

She was an excellent cuisinère and we enjoyed a superb meal comprising several individual courses, all beautifully prepared. The meals we continued to enjoy during the remainder of our all too short stay were of a similar high standard.

Seated at a nearby table was a senior French police officer, who, apart from exchanging simple basic courtesies, such as "Bonsoir Messieurs, bon apetit," and later, when he left the room, "Bonne nuit, dormez vous bien," made no further attempt to enter into conversation. We could hardly believe our good fortune.

The following morning, without attracting any untoward attention, we walked through the town to the railway station to enquire about trains to Algeria and found there was no train to Souk Ahras for the next two days. We booked third-class tickets in advance and returned to our hotel where we spent the time relaxing, making the most of the hotel's catering and comfortable beds, our last luxuries for two years to come.

We decided it would be advisable to stay in the hotel rather than risk exposure in the streets. The possibility of being recognised as escapees from Le Kef by Vichy military personnel or members of the Gendarmerie was foremost in our minds. It surprised us that we had not been approached by these authorities and could only assume they had not been notified of our escape. The route we took to Souk El Arba was no doubt not even considered by the military personnel at Le Kef. It would seem they believed we had escaped towards the station with the intention of travelling by train to Tunis. Under the circumstances, this would have been quite impossible. How they could imagine we travelled by train baffles me. The route from the caserne, as we observed, when we hid for a while on the hillside off the Souk El Arba road, was combed by soldiers. The station at Le Kef and trains scheduled to depart for Tunis would have been thoroughly searched.

There were few residents in the hotel. They and the diners took not the slightest notice of us and fortunately made no attempt to talk. Nevertheless, the wait on the station platform at Souk Ahras two days later seemed an eternity.

It was not until we boarded the train at Souk El Arba we discovered that only the lower-class Arabs travelled third-class. I was surprised now that the French lady at the station booking office did not show surprise or query my asking for third-class tickets. We were very conspicuous and promptly moved into an unoccupied second-class compartment, where we stayed undisturbed until the ticket inspector arrived. He accepted my explanation of our mistake and issued a supplementary ticket without any query. I still have this ticket, retained for nearly sixty-eight years.

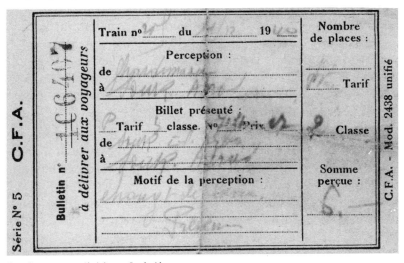

Supplementary rail ticket to Souk Ahras

Quietly, we relaxed, still undisturbed, taking in the changing aspects of a waterlogged countryside as the different scenes unfolded. We saw signs of how the poverty-stricken Arabs prepared to survive on meagre crops often grown on steep hill slopes bordering on forty-five degrees. At this time of year the anticipated produce was not visible, the growing season would be extremely short. What other subsistence could they depend upon? Perhaps the proverbial couscous and macaroni?

On arrival at the Tunisian/Algerian frontier all passengers had to leave the train and queue on the platform for an identity check. We remained in our compartment, which was immediately opposite the spot where the official was carrying out his check and at the same time eyeing us with suspicion. This was certainly the time to make a decision. What decision? Fortunately, we were not required to make it, it was made for us. Our problem became resolved quickly and unexpectedly when two French Military Policemen appeared in the corridor and opened the compartment door. One of them asked quite cheerfully, "Permission militaire?"

My simple reply in the affirmative satisfied him and wishing us both a good vacation he closed the door and the two departed. The official on the platform witnessed this and took no further interest in us. The passengers reboarded the train and by early evening we arrived with no further incident at Souk Ahras, only to find our connection to Algiers had left five minutes earlier and there was no other train until next day. This led to our downfall. It had been our intention to board a train using platform tickets and subsequently elude the ticket inspector. Having observed how the inspector operated on the train from Souk El Arba we considered this to be quite feasible. Sadly, we never had the opportunity of putting it into practice.

Now short of money, we took to the road again, hoping we might find some sympathetic French civilian who would give us shelter. It was becoming dark when we made our first contact with a man, who appeared to be well disposed when we spoke to him at his garden gate, in the light from a nearby street lamp. On hearing our plight he showed sympathy and was apologetic but unable to take any risk. We were soon to learn that the man we believed to be sympathetic was an Italian. We watched as he quickly went indoors and could see through the glass-panelled front door in the lighted hallway him reach for a telephone. This immediately roused our suspicion and we discovered later he had phoned the local military bureau.

Mistakenly, we took the road ahead out of the town. From this road there was no place to hide. Nor could we climb off the road, up or down, the terrain shelved too steeply on both sides and the ground was a quagmire. We should have doubled back smartly, sought the side streets in the town and enquired again for help. Surely we could not be so unfortunate a second time. However, the opportunity did not arise.

Shortly afterwards we were trapped, caught in the powerful headlights of two military vehicles carrying armed personnel, who leaped out clicking back the bolts of their rifles and screaming for us to halt. We were frisked unceremoniously for weapons we did not possess and bundled into the nearest vehicle where we re-encountered, now in hastily donned uniform, the well disposed looking man from the garden gate. He was a French speaking Italian from the Deuxième Bureau, which collaborated on behalf of the Vichy French with the joint German Italian Commission, now absolutely in control of French North Africa. It was he who had reported us by phone to the authorities, and a few minutes later, back in captivity, we were locked in cells at the Souk Ahras military barracks.

Next morning we were taken to a military bureau and interrogated by a man of gross physical proportions who spoke fluent English. Employed by the Deuxième Bureau, his main interest was to discover how we had travelled from Le Kef to Souk Ahras. In spite of astute questioning he appeared satisfied that it was by train from Le Kef via Tunis and we made no attempt to disillusion him.

I asked if, as escapees having crossed the frontier from Tunisia into Algeria, we could stay in the caserne here at Souk Ahras. With no hesitation he answered simply, "ABSOLUMENT PAS," ("DEFINITELY NO,") and went on to explain in very good English that Le Kef was the belly button of the world, to which we were attached inextricably by the umbilical cord, which would not be severed until the Allies were defeated. It should not take long!

"After that?" I asked.

He shrugged his shoulders, levered his huge frame laboriously out of the chair and left the room.

Q. "Qu'est-ce que nous pouvons faire?"
A. "ABSOLUMENT RIEN DU TOUT."
Q. "What can we do?"
A. "ABSOLUTELY NOTHING."

Surprisingly, we were not taken back to cells but to quite a large barrack room with heavily barred windows. Here we spent the next three days in relative comfort. The food was of a far higher standard than that at Le Kef and although locked in this room, we had permission, accompanied by guards, to go to the cabinet whenever necessary.

On the second evening we experienced an incredible and completely unexpected surprise. The chef de poste responsible for our guards was a French speaking Arab adjudant chef; a rank that I explained earlier is the equivalent of our warrant officer. He invited Ted and me to join him and his fellow French and Arab senior NCOs in their sous-officiers' mess for drinks. It was here I introduced him to the United Kingdom university sconce drinking, a penalty for offence against table etiquette. On the wall of the mess was a long highly polished brass trumpet, rather like that used by postilions in the days of coaches and horses. I don't know if it held a yard of ale, it certainly held a pint of beer that surprisingly was available in the mess bar. Each sous-officier was required to drink one sconce in turn without stopping. We had a hilarious 'one off' evening and with the deepest apologies the chef de poste had to lock us back in our room after the session. I found a bottle of red wine under my pillow!

Not all the military were pro Vichy. This is what concerned the Vichy hierarchy.

Our journey back began early on Saturday morning. It was to be in stages taking two days, firstly by train from Souk Ahras to Tunis and then to Le Kef under the escort of a French Army lieutenant and two Arab guards, who never left our compartment.

During the first stage of our journey the train stopped at the Algerian/Tunisian frontier. This was the station, where about ten days earlier, Ted and I had fortuitously crossed without detection; thanks to the two French Military Policemen, who had asked if we were on "permission militaire"? It was the same man at the checkpoint who had examined the identity cards of passengers on that occasion. The expression on his face was of combined incredulity and apprehension, when he recognised us. Perhaps he thought we would inform on him! Although feeling terribly depressed, I could not resist the temptation of smiling and closing my left eye in a controlled wink that asked the unspoken question. "Do you remember me?"

It was a long and tedious journey. We were not allowed to speak to other passengers, many of whom viewed us with surprised curiosity.

On arrival at Tunis on Saturday night the snow was falling quite heavily again and the lieutenant's orders were for us to spend the night in military cells. He assessed the appalling conditions and very generously, at great personal risk, as his family lived in occupied France, offered us an option. If we gave our verbal parole not to attempt an escape for ten hours, he would arrange our hotel accommodation for the night in a room adjoining his, but with an armed guard in the corridor by our bedroom door and another posted outside below our bedroom window. It was a magnificent gesture from a true Frenchman, who had an invidious duty to carry out. No way would we have broken faith with this officer and gentleman, so far removed was he from those bastard 'Vichyites'.

After an excellent night's rest in clean and comfortable beds, we enjoyed a breakfast of coffee and croissants with him next morning. Payment for this and the cost of our hotel accommodation was all settled out of his own pocket.

On leaving the hotel our paroles were withdrawn immediately. We were taken to a large military bureau in the city for completion of documentary formalities requiring the Lieutenant's attention. It was whilst waiting in this large bureau I set eyes on her. She looked so typically French; a slender graceful civilian girl, aged about nineteen, who left her desk and walked slowly towards me. We never took our eyes off each other until she threw her arms around me in a tender, amorous embrace. There was a pause as she whispered her name, "Toussainte". The few moments of idyllic bliss were shattered rudely by one of the guards as, with the butt-end of his rifle, he pushed me away, murmuring, "Défendu."

Toussainte was not to be thwarted and very deftly, using a sharp pair of scissors from her desk, snipped off an RAF button from my uniform tunic. She whispered, "Souvenir", as she kissed me and before we were finally bundled out of the bureau, surreptitiously pressed a small folded note into my hand again whispering, "Ecris" ("Write to me")

We were taken to the station where there was a long cold wait on an exposed platform. It was here we met a charming elderly French professor and his daughter. They spoke beautiful French, so different from the idiomatic slang spoken by most of our military guards. I found it so easy and pleasant to converse with them. Understanding each other presented no problem and they were completely disbelieving when I explained the conditions under which we lived and were housed and treated in the military caserne at Le Kef, about which they had no previous conception.

The professor gave me a splendid book on the composition of French business correspondence. It was a book he had prepared himself and which I found most informative. I learned later in the prison camps how to say in French, "Yours faithfully and assuring you of our best attention at all times" etc., in many formats! There was great sadness on the faces of father and daughter when we shook hands and said our goodbyes. I often wondered what they would tell their families about their encounter with two young English airmen. It was ironically sad, that under such incredibly unjustifiable circumstances, I should meet the beautiful Toussainte in the morning and the delightful young daughter of a French professor in the afternoon of the same day. The armed Arab guard and French lieutenant, to their credit, had stood by patiently, not interfering.

The time had now arrived, when they accompanied Ted and me very closely to the awaiting train that was to take us back to confinement and captivity. Can the outcome be imagined of what would have transpired had Ted and I attempted to make a break? IN THAT EVENTUALITY I SHOULD NOT BE WRITING THIS SCRIPT.

It was another cold, long and tedious train journey from Tunis to Le Kef. The snow, which had ceased earlier, began to fall again and the train stopped at every station. Many of the passengers were middle class Arabs travelling barefoot, mindless of the cold and the encrusted snow that melted on their feet in the relative warmth of the compartment. The women wore yashmaks, over which they peered at us in curiosity with those large brown eyes. Passengers seemed indifferent to our guards, who to their credit remained as inconspicuous as possible.

The weather was dreadful when we reached the station at Le Kef and we were taken quickly, under new guards, to a different section of the military caserne. It was here the lieutenant left us, his sad mission completed. We never met him again. He was indeed a true gentleman. A French gentleman, I shall remember always for thoughtful and kind understanding, at a time of adversity for us both.

Cells and dungeons formed a part of this caserne and for centuries they had served the purpose for which they had been intended. Ted and I were bustled unceremoniously towards the dungeons where we finished in solitary confinement. My dungeon stank and from the light of the guard's torch, before he slammed the heavy iron door closed, I noticed a filthy blanket on a large stone slab. My bed for the night! I remonstrated,

"This is a horse blanket." "The horse doesn't mind," he replied. With these words he slammed the door and I was in complete darkness.

I had never experienced enduring complete darkness before, a condition to which my eyes did not become accustomed. I had to feel. There was no amenity so I urinated on the floor, as others had done before, then from pure mental exhaustion, fell asleep on this cold damp stone slab under the cover of the stinking horse blanket. Poor Ted Hart in the next dungeon was experiencing exactly the same privations.

How low could these evil Vichy French bastards sink?

It was difficult to keep warm and the loss of body heat caused me great anxiety and discomfort. Not knowing the length of time we were to spend under these conditions compounded the problems. What did our captors believe they would gain, from what was none other than a blatant offence against young humanity? They represented a scourge against recognised decent behaviour. At best they were unadulterated scum!

Our states of mind must have been in complete turmoil and disarray. Looking back over sixty-seven years it is difficult to reconcile the mental and physical abyss into which we had been subjected as penalty for doing our duty. I did not mention these circumstances when writing home to my parents fearing the terrible distress it would cause. In fact it is most unlikely that mention of the dungeons in correspondence would have passed the Vichy French censors.

We remained in dungeons for two more days. 'La soupe' was brought to us by armed guards and served in filthy army gamelles (mess tins), visible to me in the guard's lamp when it arrived. Fortunately, I could not see the contents in the pitch-blackness that followed when he slammed the doors closed again and had no idea what I was consuming, although it tasted vile. The noise of the slamming of those doors will remain in my memory for the rest of my days. It created an almost indefinable terminality.

There was no communication between Ted, myself and the guards when they brought 'la soupe'. They remained completely taciturn and refused to answer any questions or express any opinions during the brief time between entering and leaving the cells. We lived in a lost world. There is no definitive expletive word in my vocabulary to describe adequately my contempt towards our captors. However, we survived. On the third day we were taken to a military bureau in the caserne where ex captain of the Hudson aircraft Flight Lieutenant Cooper, now our British CO, was waiting.

We were paraded and stood to attention before a smug French Army Captain who, seated behind a large desk, was trying to put on an imposing presence. (It is surprising how a large desk creates a feeling of importance for those sitting behind it). Flight Lieutenant Cooper stood at our side facing him. He explained in French that we were not criminals but prisoners of war doing our duty in escaping and did not deserve the imprisonment in dungeons, to which we had been subjected. This made no impression on the man and by now, Ted and I were showing our feelings by body language expressing resentment, which did not escape his notice.

Captain Cooper, as we called him, quickly reminded me that the Frenchman did not like my attitude. "Tell him I don't like his," was my instinctive rejoinder in English.

"Watch it Hudson," Cooper replied, "I am trying to get you both out of those dungeons and he is perfectly capable of sending you back, where you could die in these conditions."

Our CO was right of course, so with reluctance, we behaved more correctly in front of this out and out Vichy bastard and were returned to our original quarters, where we were confined for fourteen days, with all so called 'privileges' withdrawn. That is how we spent Christmas 1940.

The welcome back by our fellow prisoners was neither cordial nor sympathetic. They showed their resentment of our return by effectively, 'sending us to Coventry'. For a while we were completely ignored, which created a most non-Christmas like atmosphere. It was as though we did not exist. Sadly there was no escape from this positively hostile situation. We were herded together in an overcrowded, filthy room and I wondered with apprehensive dismay what the New Year 1941 had in store. A great strength of purpose was required to be resolute. It was the saddest and most unpleasant Christmas I have ever spent.

• • • • • •

Early in the New Year Toussainte and I began an exchange of letters, her letters to me were a comfort and great joy in those dark days. Then I received a third letter from Tunis, written by a friend of her family at the request of her father, forbidding any further communication or contact with his daughter and requesting me to destroy her letters. In view of the difficult situation in which decent French citizens were placed under the controlling German Italian Commission, he felt his family could become under suspicion and at risk. With sadness, I complied with his wishes regarding correspondence and did not write to his daughter again but retained her letters. A precious and short relationship ended and I never heard from Toussainte again.

Letters from home began to arrive. I heard from my parents that on 23rd September 1940 they had received a telegram from RAF Records Office, Ruislip, informing them that I was safe in Tunisia.

The first Red Cross food and clothing parcels began to arrive and became our salvation. They were received with the utmost gratitude and appreciation by all prisoners and throughout my entire term of imprisonment continued to reach us. Words are almost inadequate to express the sincere thanks from all of us, to The International Red Cross and to all others, who in the cause of humanity, helped to alleviate our sufferings.

Tunis le 2 11/40.

My dear friend,

I could receive your news. You are very. kind not to have forgetten me. I had thought that it would have been only an interview and no more. I thank you for all you wishes, you sent me. I also send you my wishes for the new year.

I hope that the year 1941 will bring the end of the war, and will permit you to go back to England, to find again you family and all the people you love. I hope also that all you wishes will be realized.

I hope that the christmas night has not been to much desagréable. and that you could have receive news from you parents.

I keep allways with plenty care the button you gave me, and I can assure you that I shall not loose it. It has for me much more value than you give to it.

Do you not forget when it will be possible for you, to send me your insigne of the R. A. F. I would be so happy.

You ask me a photo. It is desagreable for me to send you it now. You understand, that I would prefer to wait that you are in England, if you will think still to me.

You can in the meanetime send me one of you photos with great pleasure I would receive it.

The days might seem to be long for you. I hope that my thought (I think often to you) will render those days not to much des agreable.

I will not be angry if you do not write me often. I understand quite well.

I am late to reply you, please excuse me, but I will write you more in the future.

With much kindness.

T--------e

XXXXX.
XXXXXX.

J'espère que vous me comprendrez.
J'écris bien mal –

Letters from Toussaint who I met briefly in military bureau Tunis after recapture from Le Kef escape

Tunis le 18 Févri 1941

cher camarade -

I am late to reply
to your letter, in order not
to change. I am lucky to
know that you are satisfaid -
the last news, which you recei=
ved from england have surely
brought to you all the satisfaction
you were waiting. I hope for
you that you will receive such
news very often., You must
learn to be patient and to
wait - You OKay at le
Kef is not so desagreable. you
told me that you have passed
good evenings there.

the temperature must be
cold enough there, but you must
have the habit of it. you have
surely seen the snow, here we

never have seen it - the temperature
is a little bit better here now
happily for me, as I don't like
the winter - Do you take walks?
you will have soon the pleasure
to appreciate our nice sun

    I thank you for the compliments
you give me. But I know surely
english much less than you know
french, you can be sure.

    I regret that you have no
photos to send me.

    you will think to me, when
you will be back to england and
I hope it will be in short time.

    I keeps allways my dear
button in the meanetime, waiting
your insign of the Raf.

    It is a little difficult to speak
of me. I fear allways the control. there
in tunis, there are no distractions
since the war. but I hope that
better days will not be long to come
also for you - you are of my opinion,
indeed.?

will think to me, I hope also that you,
you can come back later in Tunisia.
if in other conditions

*Je m'en vais terminer ma lettre en
français. Je n'ai d'ailleurs guère de
chose à vous dire - J'espère avoir très
bientôt de vos nouvelles - en attendant
je vous envoie toutes mes amitiés.*

T -- T -- n e .

┌──────────────┐
│ † x α x α   │
│ x x α x α †   │
└──────────────┘

Tunis the 1st March 1941

The young girl, to whom you have written
some letters, asked me to write to you, in order
to ask you not to write her any more. She
has had some troubles in account of such
correspondence at home, and she can not
reply in the future to your letters. Please
do not write her any more, and excuse
her of such demand

A friend of her

This letter speaks for itself

MÉDÉA

· · · · · ·

*There are special rules, understandings and ethics, pertinent to all
escape procedures. In most prisoner of war camps there will be an
escape committee to be consulted by any prisoner, or prisoners who
are planning an escape. Normally approval will be granted only
if a specific plan does not jeopardise a larger or more important
undertaking. There have been exceptions, when suddenly unexpected
on the spot opportunities have arisen, enabling a man, or men to
evade camp. It is the duty of all prisoners of war to try and escape,
if not prejudicial to others. It is their duty also to cause harassment
and problems to their captors, to tie up enemy manpower. During the
course of my imprisonment, as you will learn from later pages, I spent
weeks in cells in consequence of such behaviour. These experiences
were not enjoyable but in some respects were rewarding and gave me
satisfaction.*

· · · · · ·

At the end of April 1941, quite unexpectedly, we received
unbelievable news of good fortune. We were to be repatriated in
exchange for prisoners from a German submarine crew. Whilst
negotiations were taking place, we were taken by train from Le
Kef to Algiers and thence by road to Médéa, a pleasant small
town in the mountains south of Algiers. Here we met up with
a small number of army privates who, after the fall of Dunkirk,
miraculously found their way to Marseilles and crossed the
Mediterranean to Algeria. Although it was still neutral, 'Maréchal'
(Marshal) Pétain had established his Vichy government and the
poor fellows found themselves behind prison bars; another Vichy
malaise that defies description. What was in the mind of this
infantile, immoral Pétain and his subjugated moronic 'yes men'?

Now the soldiers, who had been imprisoned in an Oran civil
gaol, were released and shared accommodation with us in a small
hotel in the centre of Médéa. Although we slept crowded, three
in a single room with three beds, we were all free. There were
no guards and each day the hotel provided a light breakfast and
two main meals of a decent standard. As aircrew we received a

small monetary allowance enabling us to buy drinks in the local café bars. It was here I met Daffy Watson, an army private of great physical and mental stature. We became close friends after I offered to buy him a drink when he had no money to repay. At first he refused, such was his pride, but after further persuasion I prevailed upon the big fellow to accept. More about him anon.

I became friendly with a little Arab French young lady who lived and worked in the hotel. She was married to a member of the kitchen staff, was bilingual and spoke Arabic and French fluently. Being very petite and about seven months pregnant her lack of height was accentuated. She was like a cute big doll and always referred to me as 'Dooglass'. One morning she produced a letter and asked me to read it. To my surprise I found the letter, which was in French, very personal to her and in consequence suggested she should read it herself. "But, Dooglass, I can't. I cannot read nor write," so I read the letter to her several times to make sure she understood its contents. Then at her request and to her dictation, I somewhat laboriously managed to write a reply. It is not easy to handwrite in another language to facilitate interpretation.

The next few descriptive passages are not intended for the prude or those who seek shelter under the cloak of hypocrisy. If they are prepared to broaden their minds and come to terms with realism, then read and absorb. What follows is of the real world.

I am sure most readers will be aware there is a red light district in most French towns. As we were young servicemen, recently free from inhospitable captivity and now raring to go, we had an enquiring curiosity to learn more about our environment and what it had to offer. Our enquiries soon guided us to what allegedly was one of the better brothels. A bordel that not only provided scope to enjoy feminine comfort, but also had a well stocked bar of quality wines. We anticipated our stay would be short, prior to repatriation to England, and quickly took advantage of an opportunity that appeared too good to miss. Heading off in the right direction, Tony Randall, Ted, a few others and I had no difficulty in locating our 'maison'. Three of us stayed together, but being more accustomed to simple French speaking, I took the lead.

The Frenchman who greeted us was presumably the proprietor and the brief introductory conversation, which was in French, when translated went like this: -

"Good evening gentlemen, how can I help?"
"Three house red wines, if you please."
"Certainly sir."

He served three glasses of superb red house wine at a very reasonable price. There was no obligation to patronise the place for its brothel services and in this context he made no attempt to influence us. Many people patronised it simply for the quality of the wines.

The brothel set-up reminded me of that depicted in American Westerns. A mirrored brightly lighted bar displayed wines, brandies, eau-de-vie, absinth, anisette and several short aperitif type drinks. There was quite a spacious floor on which the French and Arab girls, who in reality were women aged probably between twenty and forty or older, circled and offered their services quietly and courteously to prospective clients. They spoke mostly in French, although the Arab girls spoke their own language to Arab soldiers. A stairway led from the ground floor to a balcony with en suite rooms off, from which the girls provided their services.

Everything was well conducted and all the girls were clinically and fully medically examined once a week. We soon discovered the location of the surgery where these medical examinations took place and were told the safest time to approach a girl was immediately afterwards. It was not uncommon for a girl to accept a client promptly following her examination. The risks of infection were well documented and understood.

On arrival at the brothel, Tony was approached by an Arab

girl who took him to her room. We learned afterwards that his decision was not unwise as most of the Arabs and Arab soldiers went with the French girls. I was promptly approached by a French woman who would be about forty years old. She spoke intelligently and was dressed in a long openly divided black gown. We conversed in French and I became very genteel when I suggested she might like a drink. The barman knew exactly the drink she required, which he produced before I had time to ask. She went on to enlighten me that the cost of her services to me would be ten francs and the same for my friend. Ted suggested we tossed as to who should go first.

It became my doubtful privilege. With some trepidation and apprehension I followed my hostess upstairs to her room and wondered if I was making a mistake. It was then she slipped out of her gown and apart from retaining her brassiere she was completely naked. Seated on a bidet, with legs wide apart, she began sluicing her body with a medicated liquid. "This is for health reasons, you understand Monsieur". Yes, I understood and was required to do likewise.

I would not describe the experience that followed as really enjoyable. To her it was simply another job carried out courteously in the course of a day's, or should I say evening's work? Ted followed.

Ted and I took the precaution of providing our own early treatment by applying a strong solution of dissolved potassium permanganate crystals to our bodies. The stains took a long time to disappear. Should any infection have resulted we understood that it took a week for symptoms to become manifest. It is highly probable that our anxieties in this context were quite unfounded, nevertheless, the passing of a week appeared to be an eternity, but all turned out well in the aftermath.

We revisited the brothel to enjoy the excellent wines. My hostess came up to chat and made no attempt at coercion after I explained our visits from now on would be simply socially friendly and to enjoy the wines. She understood. I bought her drinks and we had long conversations during which she told me about her family living in occupied France and expressed a real anxiety for their safety and well-being.

I observed the other women in the brothel as they contacted potential clients and if successful disappeared with them to their rooms. They led a sordid life. It had been an enlightening and in many respects almost a humiliating experience of sophistication for me. It opened my eyes to the sad life of women earning a living by exploiting the frailties of masculine desires. My woman was a good conversationalist. I say this in sincerity. She was an intelligent and charming lady earning a living in a dubious way. The prude, and those who lead a life sheltered under the cloak of hypocrisy, may be critical. So be it.

Wilbur Wright the wireless operator air gunner from the Lockheed Hudson, and Ted Clayton evader from Northern France at the time of Dunkirk, visited a friendly French family in Médéa, where they played pianoforte duets together. Leading seaman Pickles, not being indifferent to his vocal prowess, would accompany them in baritone song to entertain their French hosts. The master of the house was a senior gendarmerie officer and a highly respected man by the local residents. In his many duties he was required periodically to inspect the town's brothels. Pickles misguidedly chose the wrong time to pay his own personal visit to one of these establishments. It coincided with the gendarme's official visit of inspection. Needless to say, Pickles did not enjoy future opportunities of flexing his vocal cords in the master's house!

Occasionally, Tony Randall, John Riddick and I visited an English lady and her two sons about our ages, at Dormiette, just outside the town on isolated hilly countryside. They were obviously conscientious objectors and led a frugal existence living in tents. I do not know how they became accepted and allowed to live under such conditions, nor from whence they came, or how they arrived at Médéa. We were encouraged to visit and were rewarded by regular drinks of tea, which tasted of smoke from water boiled on an outdoor smouldering wood fire.

Goodness knows where they got the tea. As far as I recollect it was unobtainable locally. Were it not for the International Red Cross, it would have been a luxury we had not enjoyed since leaving England. These people repeatedly preached pacifism and urged the importance of our not returning to hostile flying that would result in killing Germans. How they would continue to survive in winter, under what would become uncomfortably chill conditions, I don't know. We never did know. We were moved on, as you will soon discover and never met them again after leaving Médéa.

Tony Randall and I later frequented a small and intimate Café bar in the town that I shall not name on ethics principles. It sold good quality wines and offered other facilities we elected to forgo. Madame fell in a big way for Tony and suggested I could be comforted by her attractive young Arab hostess. That I would not dispute. Instead we sought a café in the town centre, I believe called Café de la Place, patronised by the more genteel middle class residents. It was in here Ted Hart and I met two attractive young French girls, Marcelle and Andrée, with whom we became friendly and spent many pleasant evenings together. The girls' inability to speak English presented no problems; sign language being universally understood proved to be a useful substitute!

Our rendezvous in the bar most evenings was followed by enjoyable walks in quiet country lanes. The surrounding mountains provided a background of scenic grandeur. An opportunity to investigate the secrets they concealed did not arise. The habitats of the animals living there were guarded by the animals and protected by them from man's intrusion. We never encountered the jackals, wild boar, wild cats and snakes whose domain was secure, although occasionally an animal would stalk unmolested into the town.

We were at unrealistic peace with these two charming French girls and lived temporarily in semi paradise, inconceivable, after the traumatic conditions we had endured in the barracks at Le Kef, and the conditions we should soon experience again.

One evening they failed to arrive at the bar as was customary and we were approached by an older woman who was quite upset when she spoke to us. She carried a message from the girls' families forbidding them to have any further relationship with us and for the same reasons as Toussainte's father. Below is my translation of the last letter I received from Marcelle in Médéa, dated 28th May 1941, a few days before we left for Aumale.

It is a sad letter, which tells its own story about a short, harmless and friendly relationship between two young French girls and two young English airmen. The girls were the charming daughters of two decent French families. In their hearts they bore no grudge towards the young Englishmen who fought with their French counterparts at the beginning of the war. I still wonder what would have been the girls' feelings, and those of Toussainte, when they were separated from the young British airmen.

Dear Douglas,
You will now have returned from Algiers and will know something about the capital of Algeria. What do you think of it, that which we call White Algiers? There is a big difference between it and our little Médéa, they are not at all alike. Algiers is the large city, Médéa the big village with all its gossip and tittle-tattle, but in spite of all that it is not too bad. I have known it for fifteen years and like it a lot.

So, a little bird has told you my name, how indiscreet!

You feel you don't speak French very well, that's not my opinion. I say to you most sincerely you speak and write it correctly enough and that I will never be able to speak and write English so well. Perhaps that is not important.

Andrée is also sorry that your friend does not understand our language and that she is not able to speak English. Nevertheless, I expect they understand each other. In spite of all that you are there to interpret.

Didn't you have your daily walk today and go to Dormiette? I seem to think I saw you go by.

I will close for today and hope you are not as lazy as I when it comes to writing. In your next letter tell me a little about yourself and what you used to do in England.

> *All my love*
> *Marcelle*

I continue with my letter this evening since I saw you and you told me earlier you would be leaving on Saturday. It can only be a sad passing moment and I hope most sincerely everything will soon turn out all right.

I know only too well that life is not easy for you, but what can you do? Nobody can do anything. It makes one a little pessimistic but don't let it get you down, put aside depressing thoughts.

I hope we can write to each other if it isn't too much trouble for you. You can write to me at my cousins' house, they will be only too pleased to receive my letters.

> *Goodnight Douglas, until tomorrow.*
> *Marcelle.*

Tomorrow never came. I thought it inadvisable to write under the prevailing circumstances. We were unable to meet and never saw each other again.

Maréchal Pétain and Pierre Laval had become clay in the hands of General Huntziger and collaborators with the Germans.

In the year 2008, I read it was stated of Laval over sixty years ago that he was the most foul figure in Paris politics, seeking for himself the prime position behind Pétain and anti British Darlan head of the French Navy.

Miliana le 28 Mai 1941.

Cher Douglas.

Vous voilà revenu d'Alger vous connaissez maintenant la capitale de l'Algérie. Comment trouvez-vous celle que l'on dénomme "Alger la Blanche"? il y a n'est-ce pas une bien grande différence entre elle et notre petit Miliana; ce n'est pas du tout la même chose Alger est la grande ville, Miliana le gros village avec tous ses commérages et ses petites histoires, mais malgré tout il n'est pas si déplaisant que ça; j'y vis depuis 15 ans et je l'aime bien.

Alors c'est un petit oiseau qui vous a donné mon nom quel indiscret !

Vous trouvez que vous ne parlez pas bien le français ? ce n'est pas mon avis, je puis vous dire en toute sincérité que vous le parlez et l'écrivez assez correctement, et que je ne serai jamais capable de parler et d'écrire l'anglais aussi bien; mais cela n'est qu'un détail.

Andrée regrette elle aussi que votre ami ne connaisse notre langue et qu'elle ne puisse parler anglais, mais je suppose qu'ils se comprennent tout de même, et puis malgré tout vous êtes là pour faire l'interprète. N'avez-vous pas fait aujourd'hui votre promenade quotidienne, n'êtes vous pas allé à Damiette ? il me semble vous avoir vu passer —

Je termine pour aujourd'hui j'espère
que vous ne serez pas aussi paresseux
que moi pour écrire. Dans votre
prochaine lettre parlez-moi un peu de
vous de ce que vous faisez en Angleterre
                    Toutes mes amitiés
                            Marcelle

Je reprends ma lettre ce soir, je
vous ai vu, et vous m'avez dit que vous
partiez samedi, je le savais depuis ce
matin. Cela n'est certainement qu'un
mauvais moment a passé, il faut
espérer de toutes ses forces, que tout
finira pour s'arranger bientôt.
Évidemment je sais très bien que la
vie ne sera pas gaie pour vous, mais
que faire? personne n'y peut rien, il
faut être un peu pessimiste et

So, for no fault of their own, these French people lived under the yoke of a dangerous and hypocritical regime, members of the Vichy government by whom they had been betrayed. They lived in fear of the Deuxième Bureau that in turn, was subservient to the German/Italian authorities now controlling French North Africa. French citizens who had relatives in occupied or unoccupied France lived in permanent fear of reprisals, lest inadvertently, they should act indiscreetly, or be considered to have betrayed their Vichy masters.

Tunisia and Algeria were still supposed to be neutral and the French became fearful of upsetting the Americans, not yet in the war. Nevertheless, Vichy French collaboration allowed German and Italian aircraft to take-off and land at El Alouina airfield. That was not to be, or perhaps I should say that did not become my crew's experience after our Blenheim crashed on 27th August 1940. The situation of the French civilians in French North Africa was getting more and more precarious.

More allied airmen joined us and overcrowding in the hotel became acute. No decision had been reached about our repatriation exchange with the German submarine crew and tension was beginning to build between us and some of the local

Oasis street scene

Typical everyday scenes in Algeria at this time. The pictures were taken by a fellow prisoner. Camel train moving South.

residents. Wisely, as we all believed, the authorities decided to move us to Aumale, where they explained, there would be more room and better accommodation.

Flight Lieutenant Cooper was assured by the authorities that this move was in all persons' interests. He instructed us to behave responsibly to enable the move to proceed without causing prejudicial incidents. We could not afford to upset the Vichy French at this critical stage of proceedings relating to our exchange with the German submarine crew, as we still believed this would lead to repatriation.

● ● ● ● ● ●

AUMALE

Our transfer to Aumale, travelling in open army trucks without guards, began in early June 1941.

In early morning, before the heat of the day, we climbed on board the open trucks in anticipation of a long, hot and dusty journey. This would take us to less crowded accommodation, pending the day of exchange with the German submarine crew, which now should not be long delayed. So we believed and became almost jubilantly excited in anticipation. Shortly after midday the trucks stopped and we all alighted and found a shady spot under trees just off the roadside. We were provided with croissants, cheese and a tasty spread in addition to a half litre of red wine per man. It all augured well. The afternoon heat was oppressive and we tired. However soon, we should all be able to relax in the relative comfort of our less crowded accommodation. Towards evening our expectations were shattered. Instantly we experienced abject disillusionment.

When nearing the town we suddenly became aware of being followed by two military vehicles carrying armed soldiers. As our trucks entered the town we noticed the streets on either side were lined with fully armed soldiers and we were driven at high speed through a large entrance into a compound swarming with guards. It was a partly tree-lined compound in which a large two storey barn-like building with heavily barred windows on both floors faced the street. Once inside this compound, the huge gates closed formidably, we were trapped. The negotiations for our exchange with the German submarine crew had fallen through. Our British CO had been deceived and we were back behind bars in a new prison camp.

To what depth of duplicity could the Vichy French bastards sink? Lower than a snake's belly was our general verdict.

The number of prisoners now approached sixty, still mostly RAF personnel. Below us, on the ground floor, was an asylum housing pitiful female Arabs, many of whom were incurably ill. Their haunting screams would often disturb us and echo throughout the night.

Thoughts of escape and how it can be achieved are certainly in the forefront of most prisoners' minds. Although it was also in the minds of our captors, they had little cause for concern regarding tunnelling from Aumale. It was quite impracticable from our incarcerated position on the first floor of the building.

Earlier in the book I described the pit of hopelessness experienced on arrival at Le Kef. There were five of us, not then overcrowded, in one smaller room. Now, after being let down by nothing short of abject duplicity, our freedom, which we believed was to be restored, had been taken away again by Vichy French collaborators. We had arrived once more in the pit of despair.

Aumale Prison Camp early July 1941

There would be some fifty, mostly Royal Air Force senior NCOs and army personnel, in one large room. We were herded together on the first floor of the building into the large room, divided by a partition to separate officers from the other ranks. There was a clearance of eighteen inches on either side of our beds but no amenities in the room. The only toilets were three stinking French squat type – we called them shit houses – which is exactly what they were. Excrement would accumulate in a pile above squat level before it was removed. I need not be explicit in my description of the situation when dysentery was frequently prevalent. The texts in the paragraphs that follow speak for themselves.

Don't be misled by the sylvan foreground façade.

In the left background can be seen the 'hell house' where all prisoners were incarcerated on the top floor. The opposite side of this building, with its heavily barred windows, faced the street.

This pit of despair was a purpose built inferno during the heat of the summer months; a prison conceived by only the Devil incarnate, or by the Vichy French. It was created to guarantee absolute discomfort with a complete absence of hygienic facilities. We ate, drank, played, quarrelled and suffered from dysentery under one roof in the same basic room.

One went to bed when the last man wished to retire. One wakened when the first man decided to get up. In between one did as I explained in the last sentence of the above paragraph. One listened to the same conversations, not always very enlightening, over and over and over again.

Aumale: - Armed guards from immediate foreground to extreme background to ensure we did not escape when being transferred from barracks to cells

The Vichy French Commandant was a swine of an officer, who would often turn up to sneer when the obnoxious swill of so called 'la soupe' arrived. He would gloat and comment loudly about the British pigs as a few inmates dashed up to be first in search of the 'choicest morsels'. On many occasions this swill would be ignored by the prisoners if a recent supply of Red Cross food parcels had been received.

The climax was reached in July after a flight sergeant escaped. On hearing the noise of rifle firing we assumed he had been shot and we rioted. He had been shot at but not killed, nor wounded. This we did not know at the time. The rioting lasted throughout the night and the guards in the street below fired volley after volley through the bars of the windows. Bullets ricocheted around the room. Remarkably nobody was hurt.

Whilst writing this text I am still in touch with ninety years old Ted Clayton OBE who was in the same room with me at Aumale during the rioting. To assure me that my recollections are accurate he relates his own experiences and tells, how the morning after the riots, he remembers finding a spent bullet in his gamelle (mess-tin). There were bullets all over the floor and wedged in the walls consequently denuded of plaster.

There was an accumulation of empty bottles in our room and many prisoners, foolishly, crept along the floor and raising a free hand holding a bottle, tried to target the armed guards who patrolled the street below. This action by the prisoners was indiscreet and angered the guards, who fired live rounds of ammunition in retaliation. Remarkably, as I have already mentioned, nobody was hurt. The street was carpeted with broken glass that the French had to clear before the street could be used again by vehicles. They tried to bully us into subjection as you can now read.

Next morning we were all marched, under the heaviest guard yet, across the town to another barracks and placed in cells for sixteen days. I shared a cell with eight others in complete darkness. Most of us developed dysentery and had to make the best possible use in the darkness of one metal churn, emptied daily by two prisoners detailed for this privilege!

The environment in this cell was not entirely conducive to creating harmony between the incarcerated prisoners. A recipe for discontent provoked unpleasantness and often resulted in disagreeable discussion. What is the end product of philosophical analysis under these circumstances? The answer is in two descriptive words, hatred and contempt for the Vichy French.

It is difficult to describe in words, stench, human or otherwise. Stomach revolting, it has to be physically experienced to be fully comprehended. Comprehension was not difficult in the above cell.

Even with a non-restricted vocabulary it is hard to find suitable descriptive words to express the unbelievable injustice my fellow prisoners and I experienced during the period of imprisonment. My ex colleague prisoners, who are still alive, would substantiate this by expressing their feelings, if they had the opportunity of speaking to readers.

Food in the camp generally was described as vile. Twice a day containers of obnoxious mess were dumped on the floor of the room for all prisoners, including officers. This description, taken from the writing of other prisoners, was no exaggeration. Again I cannot emphasise how indebted and grateful we were to The International Red Cross for their valuable food parcels.

Mid morning promenades at Aumale were accompanied by a French office and the column of prisoners was preceded by an armed cavalry soldier on horseback. Another similarly armed and mounted cavalry soldier at the rear and several armed foot soldiers accompanied us on each side, lest we should be foolhardy enough to attempt an escape.

As far as possible we would negotiate man made tracks on the sides of which were ditches, mainly dry except in certain deeper places where shallow pools of water persisted. These ditches provided natural habitats for tortoises that thrived and multiplied in large numbers. I found them fascinating. The tortoise is classed as a slow moving, plant eating, land reptile. Its body with a retractile head is encased in a scaly domed shell and thick legs provide it with great supporting strength. Those we encountered varied in size from the diminutive, no larger than a man's thumb, to the enormous like a large turtle. I have witnessed men stand on the larger tortoises, apparently without causing the reptiles any distress.

A later arrival to share with us the Vichy hospitality was a baby jackal. This little abandoned animal was rescued by a prisoner during a promenade and brought back to the camp as a companion for Raf a little black and white short-haired terrier dog. They entered into a quite uncanny friendship until, with reluctance, we were obliged to restore him to his natural environment. Latterly he could not differentiate between a playful tweak and a playful bite which became dangerous.

• • • • • •

The Vichy French officers still smarted over the Oran incident, which occurred in July 1940, an incident about which they kept reminding us. It was then that the Allies, who believed the Germans might make use of captured French warships, after due warning, attacked French battleships at Oran and put them out of commission.

About this time the French General de Gaulle raised a legion of 'Free French', who were condemned by Pétain's French government, then established at Vichy. Frenchmen overseas, in Equatorial Africa, the Cameroons and as far afield as the Pacific colonies, rallied to the Allies' cause. Any mention of de Gaulle in North Africa was 'absolument' défendu (strictly forbidden). This inspired a satirical parody.

One of the prisoners composed a few lines written in the most appalling yet descriptive French but with quite a catchy accompanying tune. It was called "Oh! Vive de Gaulle." We would sing it lustily to annoy our captors and give it our wholehearted rendering when, dressed in rags and tatters, we marched through the streets of Aumale (and later of Laghouat) on our organised 'promenades'. It showed the locals what we thought of their tyrannical Vichy masters.

This is how it went: -
"Oh! Vive de Gaulle, Oh! Vive de Gaulle
Avec son armée Française
Abas Darlan, lavez les mains
Pas collaboration avec les Allemands
Oh! Vive de Gaulle, Oh! Vive de Gaulle
Avec son armée Française
C'est la victoire pour vous
Si vous joignez avec nous
Darlan VOUS BÂTARD"
The last line was sung with a rising crescendo.

When I read the above lines, sixty-nine years after their composition, I regard them not as being in most appalling French, but as constitution of a descriptive masterpiece. In a few pithy words of expressive licence in French, the author said it all.

Again the problem of intolerable overcrowding grew and in October 1941 we left this 'Aumale Hell' and were moved to the famous, or infamous Laghouat in the Sahara desert about two hundred and fifty miles south of Algiers.

There was something inexplicably evil about the Aumale camp. It was an evil engendered by the Vichy hierarchy. It was Godless.

We were under no illusions about this move to Laghouat. We had no visions of Utopia. This would not be a transfer to an idyllic oasis.

Like all journeys I experienced when a prisoner of war in Vichy French North Africa, this turned out to be long and tedious. Fortunately, as it was October, the heat was not intolerable. The first part of the route was with armed guards by rail to Djelfa. From there we travelled in open trucks on rough stony roads, still accompanied by armed guards all the way to Laghouat. It became increasingly obvious that future attempts to escape would be fraught with dire problems. Distance and inhospitable, arid terrain completely devoid of water, held little sympathy for prospective escapers.

The futility of escape was foremost in our minds on this journey over such inhospitable territory. At first our captors gloated. The trait of the British and our Colonial and Empire colleagues was to appear as though we did not give a damn! We gave all the damns going but deliberately made light of our dreadful predicament and even made occasional feigned attempts to escape by pretending to jump off the wagons. Believe it or not, this disconcerted the guards, who in consequence could not relax and ceased to gloat. We discussed together whether it would be necessary to fence us in at Laghouat? Were we to be fenced in? Were we? I'll say we were. Read on!

This was our answer to that. We will make the Vichyites spend their taxpayers' money. Their fencing in of Allied prisoners of war will be expensive.

FROM THE ROOM WITH A VIEW

LAGHOUAT

Laghouat was a small oasis town on the outskirts of which was a large Foreign Legion Garrison. The town was basically a filthy Arab Kasbah with a small French population and a Hotel Saharienne, used primarily for those French officers who were to run the prison camp. According to a pre World War Two guide book, Laghouat was an oasis that boasted ten thousand palm trees. This was difficult to conceive! It was no consolation to British prisoners that it contained many imposing mosques and municipal buildings. From our point of view it rated as the Foreign Legion Fort it was, built to exclude intruders and incarcerate inmates. Comprised of single storey, hot weather barrack blocks surrounded by a colonnade, it served its purpose as far as the Vichy French were concerned for the incarceration of British and world wide Allied servicemen.

British and Allied prisoners occupied a section of this squalid barracks in a small compound that formed part of the garrison. This compound, encircled by a high triple fence of barbed wire, was surrounded by an even higher solid stone wall, encompassing the entire perimeter. Armed guards with machine guns were positioned strategically to ensure complete surveillance; their orders were to shoot any man who tried to escape.

The day after our arrival we were taken in small groups, heavily guarded and accompanied by a supercilious French officer, to the top of a minaret from the balcony of which we had a magnificent, uninterrupted, panoramic view of desert wilderness. Visibility extended in all directions for a hundred miles, or more.

Turning to the north this supercilious officer pointed and said: -
  "Regardez, au nord, le desert!"
  Turning east he continued: -
  "Regardez, a l'est, le desert!"
  Then to the south: -
  "Regardez, au sud, le desert!"

When lastly he turned to the west, we all chimed: -
"Yes, we know, a l'ouest, le desert!"

He had made his point.

I refer now to the question we asked each other on the journey down from Aumale. Were we to be fenced in at Laghouat? Let me examine and explain our position now in pure context.

Laghouat is two hundred and fifty miles south of Algiers. From reading my earlier text you will understand the nature of the terrain that separates this oasis town from the capital city of Algeria. Although we were prisoners of war in every aspect, our Vichy captors had the blatant temerity to refer to us as internees. As such we were described on all official documents and in all official correspondence. From what follows, does their attitude towards us, I should say behaviour towards us, suggest this?

Enclosed in the high triple barbed wire fence ran a concertina coil of similar wire about five feet in diameter. This continued throughout the entire length of the prison section of the compound. Should it have been possible to tamper with the main wire, which would have been extremely foolhardy, vibrations would be transmitted quite audibly and attract the guards' attention. Such tampering was highly unlikely as a ligne courante (continuous length of barbed wire) two metres inside prevented interference with the main fences. With the machine gun positions referred to as 'Jim Crows' sentries on the roof and with patrolling Arab Spahis and Tirailleurs outside the wire, potential escapees stood little chance. In case there were any further security doubts, our captors ensured that after dark the entire perimeter was scanned by searchlights. The Arab Spahis consisted of a contingent of native light cavalry, self-styled 'Knights of the Desert', in my opinion with justification.

Being Algerian and Mohammedan, our guards had little in common with and little liking for Europeans. This applied in particular to the Tirailleurs' force of colonial infantry.

One road passed through this oasis town, providing the only vehicular route north to Djelfa, the rail terminal from Algiers. To the south it became a winding, tortuous track leading to the oases of Ghardaia and El Golea. Ghardaia was a walled town, the military territory of which formed a part of Laghouat. Beyond, the Sahara desert stretched for a thousand miles or more towards the jungle area of Central Africa.

Throughout all seasons the desert was an entirely hostile environment in which only the itinerant Arabs knew how to survive, so Laghouat provided the Vichy French with a 'tailor made' site for the incarceration of prisoners.

• • • • • •

The Vichy French Commandant at Laghouat was Commandant Jeunechamp. Whilst serving in the French army as our ally during World War One, he received a serious injury to his right arm.

Although an ex officer of the French Foreign Legion, he was appointed by the Vichy Government as officer of the Premier Spahi Regiment to undertake the invidious task of ensuring discipline in the British and Allied prisoners' camp. It was our duty as prisoners to make his task as difficult as possible. We exercised no compromise, yet accorded the man as much respect as we believed a senior veteran officer of his calibre deserved under the circumstances. Not so did we exercise such behaviour towards the Tirailleurs' officer Lieutenant Martin, who deputised for Jeunechamp. The dislike, contempt and lack of respect were mutual, becoming an obsession with both Tirailleurs and prisoners.

I received sad news concerning the death of a close friend from The Manchester Grammar School days. Lieutenant Louis Bingham Murray, aged 23, was a brilliant mathematician who graduated at Oxford University about the time of the outbreak of war. He had been killed serving in the Royal Artillery (R.A.), whilst flying on attachment with the RAF. His mission was to investigate

Commandant Jeunechamp in charge of Laghouat Camp

and obtain a more accurate update on the effectiveness of the enemy's ground to air defences! For some inexplicable reason he was stationed in the nose of a Blenheim at the time it was forced into making a crash landing.

On hearing this news in Laghouat, through Mother's correspondence from home, I thought about the Vichy French officer's reference 'predestination' on the promenade at Aumale. Louis, being at Oxford University, was the one in four of us Mancunian friends not in the forces on the outbreak of the Second World War and logically the most likely to survive. He was the only one of us not to survive!

For the next few months living conditions in Laghouat were more congenial than Aumale. The weather was becoming cooler, the flies were dying off, we were less crowded and I shared a room with a new friend Jimmy Alexander, a six feet four inches beanpole of a man and a fellow navigator. He and I got on well together and developed a compatible relationship. This is not necessarily easy under situations of close confinement. Tony Randall moved into a small adjoining room, which he shared with a new aircrew arrival, who had been subjected to extreme exposure, having spent several tortuous days and nights in a dinghy. The effects from the sun had caused severe skin blistering and dehydration. Other members of the crew perished. This man was a regular Air Force serving member who survived the Second World War but was later commissioned and killed in a Vulcan aircraft crash.

Tony started work on a compilation to be called The Camp Echo, of which he became editor. He had no difficulty in finding talented men in the camp eager to help with articles and illustrations, and for several months I was responsible for all the typewritten work. Our little publication was always awaited eagerly and contributors increased as the weeks went by. It created a rewarding diversionary pastime for many supportive prisoners.

During the settling in period at Laghouat the thoughts most uppermost in our minds were of escape. I mentioned earlier that escape from this arid desert region was basically impossible.

Nevertheless, I say again and again, it was always the prisoner's duty to try. Firstly, contemplating escape and reflecting on the

Self, typing the Camp Echo

problems and how to overcome them is mind occupational therapy for the prisoner. Secondly, even failed escape attempts, and most attempts do fail, prevent captors from relaxing. They become unable to reduce the manpower of their guards. For them, the unavoidable consequential anxiety, presents an ongoing nightmare.

In the middle of December 1941 I developed a debilitating serious attack of dysentery. This persisted uninterruptedly until Christmas Eve, when Flight Lieutenant Cooper and Flying Officer Davies, the pilots of the Hudson aircraft, knowing of my problem, sympathetically invited me along with some of the others to join them for drinks. They had acquired a small quantity of rather

Crew of HMS Destroyer Havock

*Tony Randall - Editor of the Camp Echo
(My Blenheim W/Op AG)*

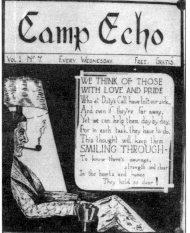

Mostly RAF personnel before the arrival of HMS Havock's Crew
Photograph taken in front of the Mark I latrine

special red wine for the occasion and 'Cap' Cooper said, whilst pouring about a quarter litre of wine into my aluminium beaker, "Drink this Hudson, if it doesn't make you better it can't make you much worse!"

It was a good quality wine and created a soothing warmth to my tormented inside. The supply of quality wine was soon exhausted. This was followed by the usual rough wine 'fortified with kerosene' that continued to flow until about midnight. We all enjoyed Christmas Eve. I felt very much better and had the best night's sleep for weeks. In the morning I wakened without hangover, nor dysentery. The 'Cap's' medicine had done the trick. I derived an unanticipated encouragement to my morale. Unbelievably, Christmas Eve 1941 in Laghouat had been enjoyable and relaxing; a direct contrast from Christmas Eve 1940 in Le Kef. There was still hope, even in a prisoner of war camp.

It was unfortunate that an otherwise pleasant evening was marred by an unpleasant incident that occurred before we went to bed. A leading seaman mistakenly accused Tony of placing in his bed a large filthy besom brush, a brush that was used for cleaning out the three so called toilets. Tony was completely blameless and had nothing to do with this stupid behaviour; nevertheless he received a nasty head and facial gash by a blow from a broken bottle delivered by the sailor. A British officer intervened promptly and the guilty attacker was immediately handed over to the French military authorities. They were more than capable of meting out punishment. This was an unprecedented action, normally the British CO would administer punishment for any prisoner's misdeed and although internal tensions often ran high, such an incident never occurred again.

Captain Dick Cooper was a British army officer who served during the Second World War as a special operations executive (SOE). He was captured from previous activities, against which charges could not be proved, and sent to Laghouat for internment as a non-lieu. He did not disguise from Jeunechamp the determination that he would attempt to escape at every conceivable opportunity. In consequence he was immediately estranged from the Vichy Commandant, who became very guarded and vigilant. He authorised the allegedly pro Pétain aspirant Rossignol, the camp interpreter, to keep close scrutiny on Cooper's activities.

Rossignol ostensibly was well disposed to the prisoners but played his cards closely. He and I talked frequently together and I tended to give him the benefit of the doubt when he expressed well-meaning towards us. As a prisoner one must never place implicit trust in any member of the captor camp.

A similar situation arose between Captain Cooper and the senior British officer, at that time Commander Bennitt, to whom he also announced his intentions of making a solo escape at the first opportunity. The Commander quickly drew Cooper's attention to the existence of the Laghouat escape committee, reminding him that it was a necessary camp ruling to obtain their sanction before attempting an escape.

After discussions between senior British and Allied officers, it was agreed that Cooper could be told about the tunnel, which obviously he would soon discover anyway. They recognised that as an SOE, his right to attempt escape had justification. He received a message from the escape committee stating that if he was so determined to get out he should join in the tunnel digging and work his passage. This was exactly what he did and openly admitted he found tunnelling experiences fraught and distressful. On one occasion he was so fraught on arriving at the face he found digging impossible. He commented on the hideous state of his mind imagining he was dead and buried in his own grave.

I have given this much thought and there is understandable reasoning behind an intelligent mind. I ask the reader to imagine being in Cooper's position at the face, say 160 feet from the tunnel entrance. If in total darkness, it would be as though you were entombed. I have experienced this dark oppressiveness. It could be that you were digging your own grave with a tunnel collapse imminent. You underwent a mental nightmare.

Captain Cooper expressed doubts whether any prison camp of the 1939-45 War, not even Colditz, was more escape proof. If the physical defences of Laghouat caserne could be pierced, a European escapee faced a trek of 300 miles of Arab country. Unsuitably clothed and unable to speak Arabic, he would be immediately suspect.

Those were Cooper's comments, every word of which I endorse completely. I said before and re-emphasize that Laghouat as a prison camp was tailor made for the Vichy French.

No further endorsement of this is really required, but I quote passages from the late Lieutenant RN John Burfield's reference as a prisoner for nine months in Laghouat.

"The chances of a successful home run from Laghouat were remote, and indeed none were achieved principally because the obstacles to be overcome were formidable.

To begin with Algeria was Arab and Mohammedan. Against this

ethnic and cultural background a European was, to say the least, noticeable. A stranger at railway stations, bus depots, cafés, cross roads, who spoke neither Arabic nor fluent French was inviting questioning and arrest. Then there was the terrain – sand, scrub and gravel, intensely hot by day and extremely cold by night. The type of barren landscape was spread over vast distances and huge areas; civilisation was concentrated along the coastal strip and the railway station at Djelfa, although perhaps only 70 miles down the road, was a somewhat too obvious place to look once an escape was discovered. Furthermore, it was assumed that two items of equipment were essential before an escape could be contemplated; water enough for eight days – the weight of this alone would have been prohibitive – and boots stout enough to withstand the punishment even short distances in the desert inflicted. When Lieutenant Martin pointed out that there was nothing out there – for once in his life he was right.

Not that these conditions discouraged several small sorties beyond the wire – and one major mass escape. Although the odds against success were long enough to discourage even the most optimistic, these attempts served two invaluable ends, both born of a determination not to be buggered about by the Vichy French. Firstly was the fillip it gave to the morale of those closely involved and secondly was the pleasure given to those less intimately concerned by the acute aggravation it caused the French authorities; both were considered by many to be well worth the 'Trente jours de rigueur en cellule' which invariably followed re-capture."

I learned by now, what took new arrivals at Laghouat a long time to discover, that it was safer, whenever possible, to avoid drinking the water and drink the wine, albeit sludge. This was contaminated with kerosene, the dregs of which were present in the barrels in which the wine was brought to us. To avoid complete dehydration, particularly in spring, summer and autumn, it was of course impracticable to avoid drinking some water. When the Red Cross tea was available we endeavoured to boil the water for making tea. That was difficult with little fuel other than tightly folded paper firelighters.

Fortunately, after my dreadful experiences with dysentery in December 1940 and December 1941, I had fewer dysentery problems during the New Year 1942 onwards. Does one become immune like the natives, after continued exposure to unhygienic living conditions? Does the body become inoculated? I assure readers that tunnel digging would have been ruled out completely for any prisoner suffering from dysentery. Apart from the obvious reasons, he would not possess the physical strength and stamina.

• • • • • •

In January 1942 the new therapy was born in Laghouat, the therapy that was to occupy several men over the coming months. For these men and for me, it was additional to the game of Bridge in helping preserve sanity. Its name was 'The Tunnel'. Although it was a project idolised by most men, it carried a great love and hate relationship. Hatred, by the very few men who feared retaliatory reprisals by our captors for any attempted escape, in a cause, or in causes, which had little hope of success. Great love wholeheartedly carried the day.

American Consul   Jeunechamp   Captain Cooper SOE   John Riddick, my Blenheim Pilot

Camp Concert

Havock Crew Barefooted

Supervised by guards the Havock Crew returning with vegetables for galley

A selection of camp concert photos

Prince & Princess Charming   *Lt (RN) Robertson's Rocket*

King and 'Ladies' in waiting   *Blessing the Witches' Brew, Ted Clayton*

Sartorially well kitted out

Sparring partners

Keeping fit in Laghouat

Also well kitted out

Laghouat chorus girls

Laghouat boxing team

Tentative digging, as a preliminary test, had been carried out by some officers from a cellar under their living quarters during December 1941. It was announced by Captain Montgomery that serious digging would begin in New Year 1942. This would bring into effect the project, which had been initially aired during the previous November, when potential enthusiasts, including myself, had been selectively approached. This news was relief from the load of anticipated doubt of wondering, which had persisted throughout the days of waiting.

During the next four months tunnel digging proceeded almost continuously combined with other important camp activities.

New prisoners arrived, initially mostly aircrew, and overcrowding did not present a problem. Tony Randall and I, with the help of colleagues, worked happily on productions of The Camp Echo. Others, under the expert guidance of Flight Lieutenant Bertie Brain DFC and his capable assistants, were busily occupied in arranging camp concerts. The mass of talent they accumulated was quite incredible. The resultant concerts were of professional standard and patronised by many of our captors including the Camp Commandant.

Under the direction of Lieutenant Commander Lamb DSO DSC and Sergeant Ted Hart, a well organised school of boxing was established that attracted many stalwarts anxious to improve their art in self defence. Yet these important activities, which induced training and discipline, coincided with the most important activity of all by a minority of carefully selected prisoners, digging the escape tunnel.

The weather in March was pleasant and although it was getting gradually hotter, we had not yet become plagued with flies and when not tunnel digging; we continued in the evenings improving our game of Bridge. The Red Cross food parcels arrived regularly and prison life was bearable. I do not wish to give the impression that Laghouat had become a leisure centre because it certainly had not, nor would it so become, as what follows will testify.

During the early hours of Monday 6th April 1942 destroyer HMS Havock ran aground off Kelibia Point on the coast of Tunisia, where she was subsequently destroyed by her ship's company. I understand that this was carried out by flooding a boiler room with diesel oil, severing the fuel feed pipes and then setting the fuel alight.

In consequence, conditions in Laghouat would change considerably to the detriment of all prisoners.

Early April 1942 bore testimony to this with the arrival of the entire ship's company of the fleet destroyer HMS Havock. To compound the problem the destroyer was carrying a large number of passengers and at a stroke the camp became overcrowded. There was no extra accommodation for this sudden influx of prisoners and the three holes in the concrete floor of the heads, as the Navy called our toilets, were completely inadequate for a camp complement now bordering on five hundred.

You will understand that the tunnel was well under way when the Havock's crew and passengers arrived. Digging was suspended briefly, for obvious security reasons, to enable our British Commanding Officer to enlighten the Havock's Captain of the tunnel's existence and what was entailed in consequence. It was important to establish a situation of understanding, discretion and circumspection, lest in the course of casual conversation, the secret of the tunnel should be given away. It never was. Security was maintained; although I am not aware of any member of the Havock's crew participating in the digging.

Shortly after the arrival of the Havock, their cooks took over the 'galley'. It was easier that way with the increased large numbers of men to feed and although the rations of food did not improve, the preparation was cleaner. I understand surprisingly, there was no salt, not surprisingly any sugar. Sadly, in early June, the Arabs took over the cooking again. One sailor reported the meals were lousy macaroni - cooked in Arab oil? What a smell! What is Arab oil?

It is alleged that prisoners of war are entitled to be victualled on the same scale as their captors. This is not my opinion as a general rule and a report with which I don't agree entirely. However, in our case, we were held by the Vichy French in Algeria and most of the soldiers were Algerian and Mohammedan. Under these circumstances we were certainly fed as the Arab soldiers. The diet suited them, but was quite unpalatable to the Europeans.

Footwear and clothing presented an ever-increasing problem as the summer heat became unbearable. Many men had to cope barefooted under diabolical situations, as illustrated by photographs in the book. Jack Surridge of the 'Havock' put his kitbag to good use making sandals. One morning, as a protest at 'appel', (roll-call) a number of prisoners were deliberately held back. The Commandant was extremely worried after the count revealed an apparent shortage of men. Later, the missing sailors appeared marching barefoot in an attempt to highlight the footwear predicament, but to no avail. Their demonstration literally fell on stony ground with the Vichy French.

• • • • • •

A dreadfully serious sanitation situation arose and work had to commence immediately digging amenity 'slit' trenches, whilst the French also hurriedly opened up new rooms in a barrack's extension. These rooms, used previously to accommodate twenty-four Arab soldiers, were required now to house fifty British and Allied prisoners of war. Our captors worked in a frenzy to increase the barbed wire fortifications.

All aircrew senior NCOs were moved from their relatively comfortable accommodation to make way for the newly arrived Royal Navy officers. I use the expression 'relatively comfortable accommodation' in the context of not being overcrowded, namely two prisoners in a room normally occupied by one French sous-officier. After the move I had to share, what previously had been a French sous-officier's single room, with six other men for the duration of my imprisonment. Under these cramped conditions I found it difficult to continue with my typewriting task for the

Camp Echo, a responsibility I handed over with reluctance to Tony Randall.

My Canadian colleague Jim Templeton and the man with whom he shared a room, New Zealander Claude Belcher, were moved into a large room that they shared initially with three other aircrew. Gradually these numbers increased. With the arrival in mid August of half the crew of the cruiser Manchester the room accommodated 100 prisoners.

Many of the younger Royal Navy officers objected to being confined in the same camp as the ratings. Ratings! I ask you? Many of us old timers, having nearly completed our second year of imprisonment, were actually by now warrant officers

Relief or occupational therapy under the surveillance of an armed guard

first class, fully qualified flying personnel with operational experience. Unfortunately, our senior NCO promotions had not been promulgated during our absence from the UK, a promotion situation that did not apply to officers. There were instances of officers with the rank of pilot officer on arrival becoming Flight Lieutenants before repatriation. During this period the opportunity to apply for commissioned rank had been denied the senior NCOs.

I, and others in the same position, found this unforgivable and inconceivable. We were regarded and treated as subordinate to men allegedly, but not in reality, of higher rank. We became subjected to the demeanour of taking their orders, yes taking orders from new arrivals, who were still civilians when we became prisoners. It may seem trivial now, but it was damned important then.

On reflection sixty-six years later, I wonder how I should have coped had my promotion to warrant officer been promulgated in February 1942, the date to which it was ultimately back dated. I should have become the most senior RAFVR NCO in the prisoner of war camp. Where would that have placed me with the Royal Navy servicemen? Should I have been responsible to the British senior officer for the discipline of all other ranks in the camp, including those of the Navy? Fortunately, such a demanding responsibility was not put to the test.

Young new naval officer arrivals continued to moan, complaining their treatment was contrary to the Geneva Convention! They were not too pleased having to share with us the same slit trench facilities under public gaze. As one wag rating put it – "They even think their shit doesn't stink but, they'll know it does when they get dysentery; that is no discriminator of rank."

For whom was the experience more demeaning; for those young officers or the 'ratings'?

Surprisingly, The Vichy French unintentionally helped advance my philosophical maturity. Life in three of their prisoner of war camps provided a series of complex experiences, unimaginable before 27th August 1940. After that, seeds sown in the fertile ground of captivity have, in my late life, as I type this, matured and blossomed to widen that philosophy.

Without any doubt the most important new arrival was Commander R.F. Jessel DSO, previously captain of HMS Legion. He sustained a broken leg when his ship was bombed at Malta and was on passage home aboard the Havock when it ran aground. This senior Royal Navy officer stood out head and shoulders above any officer I had met previously.

A brave man of fortitude with enormous strength of character, an officer and a gentleman, Commander Jessel was a true leader who commanded the respect of every prisoner in Laghouat and of whom our captors were in awe. When he was in charge at 'appel' (roll-call) the discipline of the parade was impeccable and the response to his orders, issued in a stentorian voice, was instant. We behaved like this for him and to support our British CO. By this demonstration in front of the Vichy French, they knew they would have a force of British prisoners, with which to reckon, if matters really got out of hand. Oh yes, our captors feared this man, who regrettably, was soon taken from us for hospital treatment. In his temporary absence, Lieutenant Commander Watkins, captain of the Havock, who I found to be a kind man, whom I would describe as a gentleman and an officer, assumed the responsibility of British CO.

• • • • • •

Since he joined us at Le Kef I had been friendly with Sergeant 'Wilbur' Wright, the young wireless operator who sustained serious leg injuries when the Royal Navy Fulmar shot down his plane, the Hudson, in August 1940. He had spent several weeks in hospital receiving extensive treatment for his wounds and on arrival at Le Kef one leg bore severe scar tissue from knee joint to ankle. He was a stoical little chap who exercised and made a remarkable recovery, never complaining, nor betraying any signs of animosity towards the pilot responsible for his injuries.

My initiation to boxing, and short-lived following experiences, occurred in Aumale. I mention them here because Wilbur continued to make great boxing strides and took part in several contests in Laghouat, as will become evident

In Aumale Tony Randall became interested, when he learned that Wilbur and I were going to box, and with other prisoners of different weights, helped to provide entertainment for pending visiting dignitaries from Algiers. I explained to Tony that I had no previous boxing experience, whereupon he, as an ex recreational light heavyweight, proffered advice and suggested we might go to the courtyard and practise. What a wonderful opportunity.

He explained the importance of the left arm jab. "Get your opponent on the defence with his head back and poke several short jabs at his face. This should be followed by a straight left, aimed directly at the opponent's face. He will have his guard up now, so, aim below into the plexus region. This will bring the opponent's guard down and present an opportunity to land a well-timed hook to the point of his jaw." A knockout would be guaranteed. Poor Wilbur wasn't going to stand a chance and I began to feel sorry for him.

Down to the courtyard we went and donned the boxing gloves. "Are you ready?" Asked Tony, and before I had a chance to reply he let fly with a well timed straight left to the point of my jaw. My next recollection was of lying flat out on my back on the ground, my head was swimming and I experienced an awful feeling of nausea. A very concerned Tony was bending over my prostrate body vigorously waving a towel in an attempt to revive me. For the first time in my life I had been knocked out. Slowly, I began to recover from a very positive and practical lesson, a lesson I should never forget. Wilbur, most certainly, would not stand a chance now! Tony was more upset than I. "I thought you were ready, I thought you were ready," he kept repeating. I did not enlighten him. I had been ready!

Twice Wilbur and I did engage each other in three rounds of

boxing and, with other prisoners of different weights, did entertain the visiting dignitaries from Algiers. They had come to check on our well-being and ensure we were being treated properly! That was the beginning and end of my boxing career. Wilbur beat me on points on both occasions and I am sure broke my nose in the second fight. His enthusiasm for boxing endured and whilst at Laghouat he joined the boxing school, where he received expert tuition from Lieutenant Commander Lamb, a Royal Navy Services' champion. Wilbur never lost a fight at Laghouat and if my information is correct, after repatriation, continued to box and became featherweight champion of the RAF.

He was perhaps better known in the Laghouat prison camp for his talented music playing by ear on an old honky-tonk piano; a piano that possessed more damaged than undamaged strings. He was ably supported by an RAF flight sergeant who beat a highly commendable rhythm on improvised drums. We enjoyed regular sing-songs to Wilbur's marvellous accompaniment and he was invaluable at the camp concerts. Whenever newcomers arrived from England he would ask them to hum, sing, or whistle the tunes from current song hits, which he would strum out on the piano and commit to memory. We all learned these tunes at his sing-song evenings and on repatriation arrived home fully au fait with the latest hits.

• • • • • •

Conditions at Laghouat worsened. As summer wore on, temperatures soared above 50 degrees Centigrade, in other words reaching the higher 120 degrees Fahrenheit. In the filth and squalor of the overcrowded camp, swarming flies did not discriminate between the contents of the slit trenches and the dirty tins carrying our basic means of survival, the evil 'la soupe'. The flies journeyed from the former to the latter creating a dysentery epidemic that rose to new high levels. Amazingly, I continued to remain relatively free, apart from the occasional attack of diarrhoea, which fortunately was not enduring.

In the early mornings and the late afternoons Daffy Watson

and I would exercise, gently wandering round the periphery of the compound trying to put the trials of imprisonment to rest. Although Daffy was not a scholar of literature his use of suitable expletives would paint a descriptive picture deserving of an Academy Award. He was a great man in every sense of the word. A man for whom I had the greatest respect. No harm would come to me with Daffy around.

In addition to being a tower of physical and mental strength he had an almost prodigious capacity for versatility. Temporarily, he held the title of heavyweight boxing champion at Laghouat and at the same time developed a wonderful new characteristic. At the camp concerts he became one of Bertie Brain's attractive young ladies in the front line of the chorus.

Jimmy Alexander, self, Daffy Watson   *Self, John Riddick, Tony Randall*

It was understood by all prisoners that when exercising in the compound a discretionary distance should be maintained from the barbed wire barricade. Never attempt to approach it in a nonchalant manner! Such apparent indifference could be misinterpreted immediately by a trigger-happy guard who could be capable of shooting first and counting afterwards. In the course of a game, never attempt to rescue an errant ball should it roll underneath the wire. Always draw the attention of the guard and ask for supervised assistance. This was not an act of weakness; it was an act of plain common sense. It riled Daffy, nevertheless. He would growl a string of most descriptive epithets leaving those within earshot in no doubt of his lack of affections for the Vichy captors responsible.

I have mentioned already the importance to us of the game of Bridge. After his return from hospital, Commander Jessel joined Lieutenant Commander Watkins as Bridge partner in the officers' team drawn to play against the senior NCOs in an organised competition. Jimmy Alexander and I were drawn to play against this formidable pair in a three rubbers' tournament that we approached with some trepidation. We were invited to play in the Commander's quarters where we were received with the utmost courtesy. He shared a good bottle of wine between us and it developed into a wonderful evening. Jimmy and I had the unexpected good fortune of winning the game in the last rubber, our hosts accepted defeat graciously and we returned in exuberant mood to our quarters.

● ● ● ● ● ●

Mostly RAF aircrew and three army escapees from Dunkirk! (middle row 2nd from left, Ted Clayton and front row 3rd from left Douglas)

As previously stated in my introduction to Commandant Jeunechamp and to the Laghouat camp, we were guarded by two regiments at alternating periods, namely the Premier Spahis and Tirailleurs. The photo of the Premier Spahis shows this crack cavalry regiment carrying out riding practice outside the barbed wire defences. Commandant Jeunechamp, also as previously stated, had an unenviable task to carry out that he did with as much consideration for our well being as possible under the circumstances. For this he earned our respect.

I refer again to another French officer Lieutenant Martin, nicknamed by us 'Peter the Ponce', who earlier had seen service with the Tirailleurs in Syria where he had been bombarded by the Havock. Not surprisingly, he was not too kindly disposed towards this ship's captain and its crew and never lost his vindictiveness. This was made evident one day after the arrival of Red Cross parcels, which he ordered to be stacked on the outside of the barbed wire barricade. Later, when they had been left in the heat of the sun for several hours, he ordered the Tirailleurs' guards to pierce the tins with their bayonets so the food could not be stored and used later for possible escape purposes. The contents of most tins were inedible immediately after opening. I never enquired into the penalty of an act like that or whether the Red Cross authorities were informed. I am convinced action would have been within their power. Had an escaping prisoner been captured with Red Cross food tins in his possession, I could accept the captors would have been within their rights to confiscate them.

For anyone who has not experienced the effects of malnutrition, it is difficult to understand the value of one tin of corned beef that has to be rationed between four men, who are all close friends. To avoid dissatisfaction, with its attendant arguments, we always cut cards to decide firstly, who should divide the meat into four pieces, secondly cut the cards again to determine the order in which these pieces should be taken. I have witnessed men almost coming to blows in disputes of allocation, fortunately not in our immediate circle.

Spahi Cavalry

Malnutrition affected prisoners in different ways. A few, gauging by their physical appearance, ostensibly, were unaffected. The majority lost weight and their bodies became emaciated, a symptom reflected in their sunken eyes and facial expressions. In my case it was different. From being naturally of extremely slim build, I became flabby, considerably overweight and developed a distended stomach.

My comrades teased me regularly and could not resist giving a pat to the offending part of my anatomy as they passed. They would make solicitous enquiries, asking when was it due, was I expecting twins, or perhaps triplets? It was all in fun, of course, and I took it in good part. Nevertheless, it was a physical condition that caused me concern.

Time on my hands in Laghouat, March 1942

Valuable items received from the Red Cross were tea, dried milk, prunes, butter and soap; all unobtainable elsewhere. We soaked the prunes in water; this caused them to swell and create a very pleasant juice to which we would add reconstituted dried milk. The latter was called Klim and came from the Canadian Red Cross.

A problem did arise in consequence of the process of reconstitution. This required an intake of water with the potential hazard of upset stomachs. Fortunately, my internal organs were better behaved during 1942, although prunes had a laxative reputation. There is a difference between the effects of laxative and dysentery. The prunes continued to be welcome.

Tea was most acceptable but we had to find a method to boil the water. In the height of summer, whenever tea was available, we would fill a tall enamel jug and place it, raised from the ground on two stones, outside in the compound, for heating up by the sun. At mid-afternoon, with the application of a little extra heat from a few carefully rolled paper firelighters, the water could be brought to the boil. The system was simple; it worked and was used by many other prisoners, who generally combined in syndicates of four to six men for this purpose. As there were seven men in our small room we worked as a seven-man syndicate for the purpose of Red Cross food distribution.

It was a fascinating sight to see all the containers of varying shapes and sizes dotted about the compound, unattended, for three or four hours. Never, did any prisoner attempt to tamper with these ingenious little stoves. Whilst supplies lasted, our stove helped to provide each of us with a daily one quarter-litre beaker of tea, for which we were extremely grateful.

Tea making was approached in different ways. Some men preferred to use the tea less economically and enjoy fewer strong brews. Our syndicate argued this method and compromised by making weaker brews and retaining the used tea leaves for re-use when supplies were getting low. The brews became considerably weaker but enabled us to prepare drinks in summer when dehydration was a threatening problem.

• • • • • •

It could take several weeks for letters to and from home to be received. Nevertheless, we were fortunate in being able to communicate with those at home, who were now able to send small, restricted parcels to us, containing a few essential articles. Soap was my number one priority request, and, occasionally, I received a bar of Crossfields carbolic soap from my parents.

'Dhobiing' was a word used by the navy prisoners, who joined us from HMS Havock on 6th April 1942 and from HMS Manchester in late August 1942, for washing clothes. I took advantage of my precious carbolic soap to carry out this procedure, paying particular attention to shorts and trousers in the interests of hygiene, whenever the restricted water supply permitted. During mid-summer the heat of the late morning sun was so intense that the clothes drying process was instantaneous. The first item of wet clothing would be dry and hard as a board before the next item had been washed.

There was a simple golden rule. Never leave your soap behind when you leave the washing trough; it will not be there when you return to retrieve it. This happened to me on one occasion, my whole new bar of precious carbolic soap had disappeared within a few minutes of being left unattended. I was upset and cursed man's inhumanity to man. Imagine my surprise, therefore, when an hour later, a sailor from the Havock came to our room carrying a bar of soap and asked, "Has any one of you lost this?" He was a very honest man and when I asked if he had any soap, he answered, "No, I don't have any but I thought it must be yours, you're the only chap with carbolic soap." I was deeply moved by this man's honesty and integrity and cut my precious soap into two halves. "You have some soap now and damn well deserve it," I said, handing him one of the halves. At first he refused to accept it. "No, that's yours, keep it." Finally, I persuaded the chap to take it. He was extremely grateful. I was chastened.

I shall never forget the incident of the scorpion. It arose after a sailor, horrified to discover a scorpion in his room, by some incredible piece of luck managed to catch this lethal arachnid and confine it in a bell jar. How he managed this I do not know, nor from what source the bell jar was forthcoming! We were soon to become fascinatingly enlightened by what was to follow.

The sailor explained that the scorpion used its jointed tail, bent over, to inflict a poisonous sting on its prey. If, however, the scorpion itself became cornered, it would literally commit suicide by a self-inflicted sting. He hoped to be able to prove this.

Later that afternoon he dug a shallow trench outside in the sand, forming the circumference of a circle two feet in diameter. He proceeded to fill the trench with a combustible mixture of small sticks and paper impregnated with paraffin. After setting it alight, the resultant flames completely enveloped the circle, in the centre of which, he gingerly released the scorpion from the bell jar. It was trapped and encountered a small wall of fire, no matter in which direction it ran. After repeated unsuccessful attempts to escape, it accepted the inevitable, bent its tail and committed suicide. I had witnessed an incredible practical demonstration; another of many varied and pertinent experiences in the prison camps that will never be erased from my memory.

The bell jar was used again for another demonstration after a prisoner cornered an invading snake in his room. He succeeded in placing the snake in the jar where, coiled in its cramped position, the reptile endured a few days of solitary captivity. Later, it was joined by a small lizard, captured by another prisoner. By this time the snake had worked up quite an appetite and as the relationship between the two reptiles was most incompatible, decided it was time for dinner. After stinging the unfortunate lizard into a stupor the snake slowly and systematically began to swallow its prey. Starting with the head, it continued until the whole body and tail of the lizard had been engulfed. After these exertions the snake appeared to be exhausted and fell asleep. The outline of the lizard was clearly noticeable inside the snake's body until the intestinal juices completed the slow process of digestion.

One prisoner remarked after witnessing this second demonstration, "Thank goodness, or descriptive words to that effect, we are not imprisoned in the African jungle!"

We had one small, friendly visitor, a member of the lizard family, our likeable chameleon. Endowed with a grasping tail, long tongue and protruding eyes, it was also capable of changing colour, which could create unbelievable camouflage. It was indeed a likeable little creature, befriended by one prisoner who wandered round the camp with his little companion happily at home grasping his chest under his open necked shirt. He loaned it to us one afternoon and it stayed on the shoulder of one man almost throughout a Bridge session. It had a voracious appetite and was most adept at catching flies with its long tongue, which it would flick out instantly and with deadly accuracy after sighting its prey. I never saw it miss. It never went hungry.

• • • • • •

Shortly after our arrival at Laghouat one of the prisoners rescued from further maltreatment an abandoned smooth-haired brown and white mongrel dog, which he called Wimpey. This young animal was a companion for Raf whom Wilbur had brought from Aumale and the two became inseparable. A bond of friendship developed between them, they played together and spent hours running around the camp, which was their playground. During the heat of the summer late mornings and early afternoons they would sleep, lying fully stretched, until it was cool enough to resume wanderings. In July and August, after mid morning until late afternoon, the compound would become too hot for the dogs. They would tentatively approach it from the colonnade and retreat, hastily withdrawing their paws. Remarkably, as if by instinct, they never strayed into the no man's land territory beyond the barbed wire except once when Raf needed a closer look at the Spahis cavalry display. It was quite amazing how this little dog got into position unhurt and sat in the concertina ligne of barbed wire in apparent wrapt attention. (See photo on page 105) The dogs were well groomed and kept spotlessly clean by their masters, more than can be said of many prisoners, and were the friends of every man in the camp. Feeding presented no problems, their palates were not as discerning as ours and

Laghouat - December 1941

The latrines

Ted Clayton's successful search for lost property in the latrine!

there was plenty of gash 'la soupe' to keep them alive, until one day during Lieutenant Martin's tenure, they were shot dead for no justifiable reason.

It came as a great blow to everyone. This thoughtless action saddened all prisoners and Wilbur Wright was openly heartbroken. He had ceaselessly looked after Raf whom he discovered on a 'promenade' at Aumale and rescued from maltreatment at the hands of a local Arab.

During the heat of summer 1942, prisoners occupying one of the larger rooms in the caserne suspected there was a cavity under the flagstone floor and decided to investigate. With difficulty, they managed to lever a flagstone, which revealed, not a cellar as beneath Captain Montgomery's room, but a series of water filled compartments. Discreet enquiries confirmed that these had been purposely constructed to ensure The Foreign Legion of a water supply in the event of siege and we were able to establish that this water was not being used currently for drinking. Heaven sent facilities for bathing were unexpectedly made available for a small section of privileged prisoners, of which I, as a veteran,

Prison Camp section of Laghouat Garrison

was included. It was inky dark in this subterranean swimming pool. Although the water was extremely cold, it was very refreshing and the ledges of the compartments provided useful resting places. Occasionally, the guards would make a routine patrol of the prison quarters when the flagstone would be quickly put back in place. These were quite terrifying interludes, but happily, we were never abandoned to a watery demise.

• • • • • •

THE TUNNEL

A masterpiece of domed engineering with no timbered support.

After surveying the ground above the proposed route of the tunnel, the calculations carried out by civil engineer New Zealander Squadron Leader Brickell were exemplary in their accuracy. He devised his own instruments for calculating levels, widths and distances. The technical descriptions of these instruments were beyond my comprehension. As you will read later, it was my privilege and edification to be accompanied by him in the tunnel as digging progressed, when verification of procedural decisions was required. Timber was not available for shoring and to prevent roof collapse, the tunnel had to be domed, making it effectively an arch. It required the expertise of Squadron Leader Brickell to assess this efficacy. I now describe how the tunnel originated.

Shortly after our arrival in Laghouat, Captain Montgomery suspected there was a cavity under the floor of the room he shared with a fellow officer, Lieutenant Robairre, a French speaking French Canadian, whose fluency in two languages was extremely useful. They decided to investigate. With the help of other officers, a huge flagstone was levered up to reveal a large empty cellar, an ideal place from which to start a tunnel and store the excavated sand. The officers did not divulge their find until they had succeeded in removing foundation stones from a wall at the cellar base and creating a gap sufficiently large for a man to crawl through to start digging. It was now Monty approached a selected number of senior NCOs, me included, explaining the officers' intentions and asking if we wished to help. He spoke to us outside in small groups, outlining the hazards of claustrophobia, the likelihood of roof collapses and problems of breathing that might be encountered in the confined space of a tunnel they calculated would be sixty-eight yards long. Nobody refused to volunteer. However there was no absolute guarantee everyone would be allowed to escape if the project were successful.

Entrance to the tunnel from the cellar

After very careful calculations had been made it was estimated the cellar was sufficiently spacious to accommodate the excavated sand and earth, although there was little latitude for error. The problem of lack of ventilation could not be ignored when the cellar storage space approached capacity. How providential there should be a cellar at all. It was an invaluable asset that reduced the likelihood of sand having to be transported outside and dumped in full view of the guards.

The Concise Oxford Dictionary defines the word stamina as "the ability to endure long physical or mental strain, staying power, power of endurance." In my opinion those words describe the requirements of the escape tunnel digger.

Until one has actually experienced escape tunnel digging, it is impossible to understand and appreciate the demands required to proceed without apprehension. My introduction came when I was lowered into the cellar from which the tunnel would commence. Immediately, I became aware of reality and experienced first hand the virtual impossibility of the task that faced us. This reality dawned when I viewed a jagged area in the building's foundation, from which stones in a section of the basement wall had been removed. It had taken several weeks for the officers involved to accomplish this incredible task, with the limited tools at their disposal, mainly two kitchen knives. The nearby photograph of the cellar wall is adequate substantiation of their achievement. I am not privy to know how, and by whom this photo was developed and printed. Our captors most certainly were not aware of it! As you will read later, the tunnel digging was completed by the use of two bread knives.

Initially, digging with a full-length bread knife from the face was easy and progress was relatively speedy. It was not until the tunnel had reached, say ten feet or so in length that digging became more difficult. Some men experienced the first signs of claustrophobia and became aware of the adverse effect of the tunnel's earthy atmosphere. It was as though the tunnel was already beginning to close in on them. This manifested a really serious problem with still a distance of over one hundred and eighty feet to go. The project had only just begun. Monty was realistic and offered these men the opportunity to withdraw. Some did, others volunteered to stay and stack earth and help with the hauling of the crachoirs (metal containers, literally French word for spittoons, about six inches in depth and in width slightly less than that of the tunnel. They held a large quantity of sand and by an ingenious system of ropes were dragged to the tunnel entrance, emptied and their contents stacked in the cellar). It was horses for courses. Captain Montgomery, Lieutenant Robairre the French Canadian officer and Squadron Leader Brickell had this incredible task under constant supervision.

When I started digging from the cellar wall I felt overcome by the enormity of the task and never believed the project would be accomplished. Fortunately, I was not troubled by claustrophobia and adapted myself to the unusual problems, with the exception of the first real one, lack of ventilation. The air became considerably exhausted and unpleasant. It would have been dangerous to proceed, in fact impossible, unless a solution had not been forthcoming.

The tunnel is so real and yet so unreal. To what can it be compared? It creates hope. It has purpose. It has its own atmospheres. Firstly, the excitement engendered by the knowledge of its existence. Secondly, the factual atmosphere of miasmatic, mephitic odour that becomes more intense as the tunnel lengthens. The latter is a combination of earth getting more humid and human body odour. It was our concern that this would be noticeable to our captors when they inspected the officers' quarters. Poor old Monty had to live with it. The smell lingered, even when the flagstone was replaced over the entrance. This was frequent as digging continued more or less around the clock, apart from times of appels and searches. The latter were unpredictable and often caused problems. My experiences, and that of most other diggers on several occasions, were to be almost hermetically sealed in at times. The officers quartered near the tunnel room had to exercise every precaution, and seek any pretext to discourage The French from loitering in that area.

I was suspicious when one sergeant navigator arrived who spoke fluent French. The tunnel was so important and I was convinced he had been planted. Fortunately, I quickly discovered my fears were groundless. He was a Free Frenchman who became a prisoner like the rest of us.

The importance of concealing the tunnel's entrance from our captors cannot be over emphasized. We had to be on permanent alert as they were capable of springing a sudden search without any prior warning. Although their suspicions must have been roused they never succeeded in discovering our well-kept secret. As you are aware now, prisoners working underground would be sealed below during an unexpected search. This was an unpleasant experience but fortunately never resulted in any casualties. We had to ensure that tunnel digging and attendant procedures ceased in good time before appels. Resumption of such operations always had to be withheld immediately after the roll-calls to allow our captors time to leave the prison compound. Often they would delay their departure, which in our opinion was deliberate.

Sometimes when a search took place, all prisoners were ordered to leave their rooms and assemble outside on the compound whilst their rooms were searched thoroughly. At other times prisoners were allowed to remain. On these occasions we could not resist preparing a few 'red herrings' in the form of misleading clues, or creating distractions that were not necessary. Two favourites were to glance at a picture on the wall, or shuffle uneasily over a flagstone from which surface cement had been removed deliberately. On removing the picture, our captors would find nothing hidden behind. On one occasion they went to considerable trouble to lever up a flagstone under which nothing was revealed other than a quite remarkable colony of ants. Meaningless half prepared maps leading to nowhere would be left casually on a table with an odd quite ridiculously forged identity paper. There were many others.

When digging began earnestly in January about forty volunteers took part. Not all of these intended to escape and risk the hazards of exposure in the Sahara wilderness, but they showed their true mettle by being prepared to risk the hazards of the tunnel to help others.

We were fortunate in having at our disposal the skills of Squadron Leader Brickell in Civvy Street an engineering and building contractor. He had been on his way to somewhere in the Middle East to supervise the construction of airfield runways, when the plane, in which he was travelling, crashed in transit and consequently he had the misfortune of joining the rest of us in Laghouat. Although he did not take part in the actual digging, he probably spent more time down there than anyone else, checking the progress and advising when alterations in procedure had to be made. He explained that the tendency when burrowing underground was to go upwards. If the result of this tendency had not been checked frequently, we should have reached the surface prematurely. Sometimes we would veer to the right, at other times edge towards the left. This man knew and corrected us accordingly. His advice became invaluable.

In a completely different capacity he was eagerly sought at Wilbur's sing-songs, especially if a supply of 'kerosene wine' had been accumulated. He had a well stocked library of verses, not entirely suitable for the drawing rooms of polite society. His expressive and descriptive renditions of 'Eskimo Nell' and 'She's My Girl Salome' were without peer and assured of many encores.

Reverting to the tunnel, normally we worked in pairs, one man digging at the face, the other stacking the sand into the crachoirs. Being a small person I spent a lot of time digging at the face, working three or four watches every week.

I mentioned previously that after some ten feet or so of digging, my first concern was of diminishing ventilation. As the tunnel progressed the air became so foul our home-made candles, burning Red Cross rancid butter and with wicks of pyjama trouser cords, would flicker and die. After progressing thirty yards it looked as if the tunnel would have to be abandoned, but no. Thanks to Squadron Leader Brickell and other talented officers, an ingenious ventilation tube was constructed from Red Cross empty cans with their bases cut out. When attached together they formed a flexible tube like an elephant's trunk and were carefully inserted from the roof of the tunnel through a decoy slit trench at the surface. From one of the photographs in the book, it can be seen quite clearly how the digging of an alleged amenity trench enabled this ventilation shaft to become a practical reality.

With our backs to the armed guards on the prison roof we made pretence of using these amenities, each time adding stones and sand very carefully until the trench was filled. The ventilating effect in the tunnel exceeded expectations. Instead of flickering and dying the candles blew out, a problem that was easily rectifiable, and we could breathe fresh air.

Ingenuity knew no bounds. Experts succeeded in tapping into the camp electricity wiring system and by attaching together any bits and pieces that would conduct electricity, created a most efficient lighting system in the tunnel.

One night, working down there alone completely naked and crawling towards the face on hands and knees, my backside accidentally made contact with an exposed section of wiring. I was subjected to a sudden sharp shock from some two hundred volts and this not only plunged the tunnel into complete darkness, but the whole prison section of the camp.

This caused panic among the French who thought it was the prelude to a mass escape and they were quick to locate the fault caused by the main fuse having blown. It was replaced promptly and from groping in absolute darkness, by sudden contrast I became dazzled by blazing light. The French never discovered

Ostensibly digging the 'Amenity slit trench' in reality the tunnel's ventilation shaft

Raf and Wimpey our little dogs who were shot by the Vichy French

Outside wall at extreme left of picture was where the escape tunnel came up (the prison camp occupied part of this Caserne and was 'Barbed Wired Off')

the source of the problem and normal tunnel services resumed without further interruptions. We were fortunate to get away with that experience and had to be very guarded to avoid causing a repetition. That would have certainly aroused suspicions.

I mentioned earlier the humid, earthy atmosphere of the tunnel. Digging down there at the face, even naked, was particularly hot work. The clay and sandy earth combined and became almost an adhesive on one's body. Every time I emerged from a digging stint, Captain Montgomery, waiting at the tunnel entrance, always asked most solicitously how I had got on. Sometimes digging was easier than at other times depending on the strata structure, which varied. Only once did we experience a complete obstruction when encountering a stone that was too large to remove. The solution was time consuming and involved tunnelling around the obstruction. Great care was required to ensure the correct direction and level of the tunnel was subsequently maintained.

It was evident from the earth hauled up in the crachoirs the progress that had been made from a particular session. Monty was always waiting with a beaker of wine, albeit kerosene flavoured, at hand to help slake the very parched dry mouths of the emerging diggers. A cup of tea was never available! During this period of relaxation, problems and procedure were discussed before attempting to clean up and remove the congealed 'earth pack' from one's body. This was very important and difficult. All vestiges of tunnel earth must be removed before re-entering the compound. In my opinion to this day, it was one of the wonders of Laghouat that tunnellers' reappearances after digging stints were never detected by our captors.

The tunnel was never wider than sixty centimetres and rarely exceeded that measurement in height. Consequently, it was impossible to stand and extremely difficult to turn round. One had to crawl on hands and knees to reach the face and reverse crawl back again. I experimented with dress and latterly, as the distance to the face increased, resorted to wearing an old pair of long trousers as protection for my knees. I kept the trousers in the cellar and no doubt other diggers 'borrowed' them.

• • • • • •

To the delight, and in some respects, almost disbelief of everybody who had participated, and disbelief of the sceptics who had not, the tunnel was completed after seven months hard toil.

Once opened it could not be closed for use again. It would not be possible to conceal its existence from the outside. The likelihood of it being discovered by chance could not be ruled out, so the escape committee had a difficult task. Not surprisingly there was much dissension amongst the officers, sometimes resulting in physical violence. Such was the diversity of opinions that quarrels and arguments ensued over the decision as to when the tunnel should be used and by whom. Senior NCOs had no say in these matters. It came to a head one night when a Royal Navy officer, who had expressed his opinion that the opening of the tunnel should be delayed, received such a going over from fellow officers he could not appear on appel for several days due to facial disfigurement. It required diplomacy and tact to explain this to the French and avoid suspicion.

Army Captain Montgomery held the Vichy French officers in utmost contempt and showed no signs of hiding this contempt by his behaviour at appel. He was a tall man and would stand on parade in a nonchalant attitude with his battered filthy trilby hat pulled down well over his eyes in complete disdain. When his name was called out, should another prisoner succeed in producing a loud belch, Monty's impassive expression implied that it had escaped his hearing. Of course it was done for a purpose, but how it riled our captors! He was also capable of manifesting contempt towards any prisoner with whom he was not on the best of terms. There were very few, albeit one man in particular.

At appel, prisoners were required to line up closely to facilitate the taking of the roll. When the tunnel had been completed, Monty distanced himself by a yard from an officer who had raised specific objections to an early opening. An obvious gap was created between them that did not go unnoticed by prisoners on the appel. After two days Monty had made his point and a decision was reached to open the tunnel in early June.

● ● ● ● ● ●

This sketch was prepared by Sqdn Ldr Richard Brickell, the tunnel architect, and shown to the institute of Civil Engineers after his repatriation in November 1942.

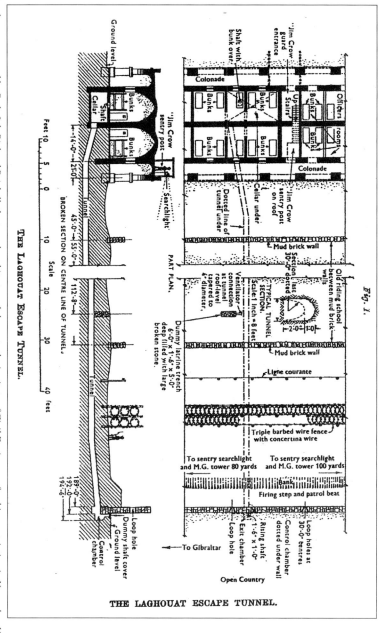

THE LAGHOUAT ESCAPE TUNNEL.

Twenty-nine men were chosen to attempt an escape. Tony Randall, Jimmy Alexander, other senior NCOs and I were included. Before our departure Commander Jessel spoke to us all extending his good wishes and adding, "If any one of you succeeds in reaching Gibraltar give this message to (he named an Admiral) saying Commander Jessel has a plan to take Laghouat." This brave man was in possession of intelligence of which we had no information, but as events turned out his plan was not put into action.

None of the escapees underestimated the potential dangers and problems that lay ahead. One of these was SOE Captain Cooper, who surprisingly chose a navy leading seaman and an army private to accompany him. These three went out together and initially headed south, hoping thereby to mislead their captors. Regrettably they were quickly recaptured.

Temperatures in early June were beginning to soar and dehydration presented the most serious hazard. After escaping, we must avoid the Djelfa road, rely on finding an artesian well and use the pathless desert tracts for the first few days. We had mapped the locations of the wells on a carefully prepared chart, copied from a special map to which we had access at the camp. The nomadic Arabs relied on these wonderfully conceived deep wells that, from a considerable depth, provided beautifully cool fresh water of outstanding clarity, perfectly safe to drink. The water was obtained by winching up a bucket from the bottom of the well to the surface. After emptying, the accepted courtesy was to return the bucket by winch to the depths below, thereby, ensuring it remained clean and available for the next traveller. It was a practice, I understand, all travellers observed. A rule of the desert.

The day for our planned departure was getting close and I had not resolved my footwear problem. One friendly RAF Sergeant Gibbins who had accepted the responsibility of becoming camp postman noticed this. His duties were to collect prisoners' outgoing letters, then, under guard, take them to the French Bureau outside the prison section of the camp, where they were censored. He would collect any incoming mail, which he would distribute to the prisoners on his return. It was on such an occasion he visited our room whilst I was trying to come to terms with an offending pair of escape footwear. 'Gibby', who was not one of the escapees, just said, "You can't escape in those Doug, take these," and promptly took off his own well soled and heeled pair of boots. The more I demurred, the more he insisted and left the room barefooted. Perhaps it was fortunate that the boots were too large. I did obtain a more suitable pair of correct size through the escape committee and returned the other boots to Gibby. It had been a wonderful gesture on his behalf. He was that sort of a man.

Our plan was to travel by night under the guise of Arabs by draping Arab style, large off-white sheets over our heads and shoulders. From a distance, at night, we should not be readily identifiable by a chance wanderer. We planned to rest by day, if possible in a scrub area, then use the sheets as tents and protection from the sun.

Water was our priority and we were fortunate in acquiring three Mae Wests (inflatable life jackets worn by aircrew as a precaution in case of ditching). We filled these with water, each could hold over a gallon, possibly sufficient to ward off serious dehydration for four days by which time we hoped to reach the Djelfa area. They could be worn like a jacket under our sheets, thereby distributing the weight. For emergency rations we each took a kilo of compressed, stoned, dry dates. I had a bottle of rough brandy called eau-de-vie (French literally 'water of life'), to be used of course, for medicinal purposes only!

Equipped with genuine identity papers in case of recapture and an issue of French francs, in notes supplied by the escape committee, we were prepared! The money was hidden carefully in the seams of our clothing, between the soles of our boots and inside rolled up cigarette papers with tobacco pressed in each end. It was never discovered.

The night of the escape in early June arrived. The positions in the tunnel for Tony, Jimmy and me were numbers nine, ten and eleven so we could not complain. These were minutes of tension and apprehension, the time when our bid for freedom had arrived. I crawled along the tunnel with my two colleagues in absolute silence, laboriously pushing my rolled up sheet and scant provisions ahead along the tunnel floor. The water filled Mae West literally weighed heavily on my shoulders and, as I was the smallest, my colleagues allowed me to go in front. My mouth had become parched already and I bit into a date stone hoping to create more saliva. I carried a small precautionary supply of these.

After what seemed an eternity, we reached the tunnel exit and climbed to the surface to gaze up into a sky of magnificent splendour with myriad stars. The pole star, our celestial compass, was visible to guide us north, the direction we wished to travel to freedom. I breathed in deeply the late evening air. It was like breathing in the elixir of life. We had broken the chains of captivity. A welcome drink of water, proffered by a naval officer who was carrying out a fantastic job of marshalling outside the tunnel exit in complete silence, eased my parched throat. Thank goodness no escapee coughed, sneezed or inadvertently spoke or called out to another escapee. That could have happened in such moments of tension.

All twenty-nine men got away undetected and dispersed rapidly into the inhospitable desert. It was surprising how quickly we lost sight of our fellow escapees, the majority of whom were travelling in a similar direction.

Beneath the canopy of a star embroidered firmamental tapestry, guided by the celestial shepherd, we trekked north throughout the remaining hours of darkness. At the rising of the sun our shepherd in Ursa Minor, also called Little Bear, abandoned the celestial compass and disappeared. We knew this navigator's friend would reappear by nightfall. In every direction we gazed into a vast uninhabited area of indefinable awesome silence.

In the early light of dawn, after covering a distance of fifteen miles, we found a suitable spot to pitch our improvised tent, well concealed, as we believed, in a small area of scrub. We had not allowed, however, for the presence of swarming ants that caused us considerable discomfort, a discomfort to become compounded by the rapid rise in temperature. The heat quickly became unbearable. I assure readers I learned a lesson from this brief experience; a lesson which would have been invaluable had I been required to escape again in the desert.

On the one hand sadly, yet on the other hand fortuitously, these hardships had not to be endured much longer. In the distance we saw and heard mounted Arab soldiers riding rapidly towards us in fan shape formation. We were captured, with no chance of evasion, by eight armed Premier Spahis cavalrymen who encircled us on those marvellous Arab stallions. The soldiers hurled abuse in Arabic as they galloped round and round raising an almighty dust and brandishing their loaded rifles. What an incredible display of horsemanship. Just when we thought our number was up they stopped, three of the soldiers jumped down from their mounts and offered us water, then, in simple French, ordered us on to the backs of their horses. They remounted, threw their rifles across to three other soldiers, who then rode back carrying two rifles apiece. They were indeed 'Knights of the Desert'. Incomparably, they rode without peer.

We were still wearing the water filled Mae Wests from which, as yet, we had not taken a drink, having previously quenched our thirsts from water carried in a spare bottle. With difficulty, I managed to fill my aluminium cup, after which I felt ill immediately. The contents were loathsome. The water was absolutely teeming with wriggling creatures. The water in Jimmy's and Tony's Mae Wests was similarly contaminated. We ditched the lot.

I made a grab for my bottle of eau-de-vie and took several long swigs of the potent liquor. The soldiers noticed our predicament and to their credit, slowed down, enabling me to pass the litre bottle to my colleagues. Between us we drank about a third of the contents.

Riding bareback on the rear of an Arab stallion, whilst holding on for dear life to its rider, as his mount galloped rapidly across the desert under a blazing June sun, was an exhilarating yet painful experience not to be emulated. We had a further brief respite when the soldiers rode up to a well, stopped and allowed us to dismount. It was our first experience of drinking cool, fresh, uncontaminated well water that lived up to its reputation. What a wonderful provider nature can be. Needless to say we made much better time on the return journey than on the way out! However our backsides became red raw and mine took several weeks to heal. My skin, which had been completely abraded, never did heal to full recovery. It is thin and tender to this day, sixty-seven years later. No medications were made available on our return to the caserne. The chafing was sufficiently severe to justify a skin grafting, which it would probably have received, had the chafing arisen through different circumstances, say at a UK home base. As I type this script I am receiving special medical treatment for a fungal infection, which I believe originated at the time to which I have just referred.

Had we not ditched our Mae Wests and been able to swill them clean and refill with well water, which was our original intention when planning the escape, would the water have remained fresh for the next few days? That question will remain unanswered.

Now was an opportunity, still under a blazing sun, to take further swigs of eau-de-vie before remounting. The contents of the bottle had been reduced to a third.

On the approach to Laghouat we were ordered to dismount and complete the last part of the journey on foot.

Entering the outskirts of the town, we made a final attempt to sing the masterpiece 'Oh! Vive de Gaulle,' as we passed to each other the almost drained bottle of eau-de-vie. Sweating, dehydrated and caked in sand we presented a pitiful sight in our filthy bloodstained ragged clothing, as we trudged wearily back to imprisonment, surrounded by eight mounted Arab horsemen guards.

We walked within a few yards of the house of a middle-aged French lady who heard our singing as she stood at the front door. She watched as we passed by and when our eyes met, buried her head in both hands, burst into tears and turned back into the house sobbing uncontrollably. I write this script sixty-seven years later and the sight of this distressed French lady is as clear in my mind now as it was then. I often wonder how she would have reacted had we contacted her immediately after our escaping when it was dark. Would she have offered us the shelter of a safe house? I shall never know but I believe she would.

• • • • • •

Alas, within twenty-four hours after departure, most of the twenty-nine prisoners had failed to evade recapture. Not one succeeded in making a getaway even beginning to approach a home run.

No heroes' welcome awaited us on return to camp, neither was there a mug of fresh tea, nor an inviting bath, instead we were taken to a colonnade awaiting the next move. When I asked the Arab guard for permission to visit the cabinet he refused and in a gruff voice said, "Il n'y a pas." Which translated literally means, 'there isn't any'. I tried again, quite politely. Came the snarled second response, "Défendu."

With venom in my voice I told him to take a running jump and get f***ed, whereupon, he strode towards me and with the butt end of his rifle knocked me flat on the flagstone floor of the colonnade. Tony Randall bravely went for the man and had it not been for the prompt intervention of a more understanding Arab Chef de Poste, he would have been shot, most assuredly. "Vas-y!" ("Go!") With those words, the Chef de Poste ushered me courteously to a nearby soldier's filthy, stinking cabinet. Then we were split up and marched to cells in another part of the garrison.

Here, I joined 'Digger' Latter, an Australian with whom I shared a single cell for the next sixteen days. We were locked in throughout this period only being allowed out into a high walled courtyard to use the communal churn, shared by other escapees, which two of us took in turns to empty. Usual cells' procedure! Fortunately, neither Digger, nor I had dysentery, a complaint to which I had been readily prone prior to January, as readers now will be aware. On this occasion such a disaster did not arise perhaps in my case, thanks to eau-de-vie, which as I said before, had been taken for medicinal purposes!

Now we had sixteen days in which to talk and swap opinions. He was a sort of dry philosopher, not easy to understand and although we differed in our political persuasions we had one common determination, make it as difficult as possible for these Vichy French bastards. Digger was perfectly justified, having arrived at Laghouat after spending seven days and nights with others of his crew, afloat in a dinghy in the Mediterranean. Sadly he did not live to enjoy the later years of life.

Whilst in cells we received an unexpected visitor, a French General, veteran of the First World War. He enquired, through the medium of a junior officer, if we had any complaints. I was not sure how to take this. Could he be serious talking to us in our present environment and asking if we had any complaints? I could have given him a string of them, but reserved my reply to make one complaint only. This surprised him and he became more surprised when, speaking in French, I answered him directly, not through the junior officer. I tried to accord him the courtesy his rank demanded and stood politely to attention, not subserviently, explaining that permission had been withdrawn for us to write letters home and our letters from England were being withheld. Surprisingly, his response was immediate and positive. He instructed his aide to ensure our rights as prisoners would be restored without delay.

I was still standing to attention, we never took eyes off each other, and in his face I peered into the open pages of a book. I don't know for whom the sadness was the greater. He was an elderly, true and genuine Frenchman, a victim under Nazi and Vichy suppression, who faced a young true Englishman, similarly suppressed under similar regimes. Within an hour we received pencils, writing material and envelopes. The General had honoured his word.

I understand from a report by one of the 'Havock's crew that this General was less civil when visiting the main camp. Apparently, he was responsible for issuing reprisals that Commandant Jeunechamp would have to ensure were carried out. They included removal of the dummy camp radio, a gramophone and cutting off the lighting. These reprisals were expected temporary measures, perfectly predictable and inevitable after a mass escape.

It would be churlish not to pay tribute to those eight young Premier Spahis Arab cavalrymen, who had held us at their mercy in the desert, with no senior officer present to control them. They had acted, using their own judgement and could have shot us dead on the pretext that we resisted arrest. No questions would have been asked. In a matter of days our bodies would have been picked to skeletal remains and quickly reduced to powder and disappeared. An organic fertilizer would have been wasted on a fruitless desert. Instead, these young men had offered us water and given us a free ride back to an imprisonment in a filthy caserne devoid of civilised amenities, but that provided shelter from an inhospitable desert. They had certainly saved our lives. May they be eternally blessed. On the morning after the escape we had not been present of course, to witness the chaotic events at appel. We learned to our delight that although Commandant Jeunechamp was in charge, it was Lieutenant Martin who was duty officer and had been on duty all night. He took the roll-call count three times, after which the French searched the camp hoping to find the missing twenty nine-men hiding as a practical joke. This was not reality; twenty-nine men had escaped and Martin was last seen as he left the outside colonnade, leaning against a wall in despair with head in hands. He would almost certainly face a court martial.

The desert, during my imprisonment years, ALWAYS claimed its victims. The escape, condoned by the majority, was criticised by some as being irresponsible and a waste of time. This I deny. It was not a wasted effort and caused considerable consternation for the Vichy French, who were left under no illusions. They had a powerful force of British prisoners to control and restrain.

They were forced to rethink. Their logistics had been thrown into complete disarray causing upset to their disposition of military personnel. Troops had to be redrafted and ravitaillement (revictualling) became disrupted due to added transport difficulties. Senior officers were charged by the Vichy French hierarchy with gross ineptitude and threats of reductions in rank. Alas, the Garrison Commander, known to us as 'The Slug', did not sever his jugular!

If, or when, one does not speak or understand other persons' languages, it is inexcusable to think they are less intelligent. It is a situation that can cause such an impression. Equally so it can apply in reverse. A situation in which I found myself regularly in North Africa but learned to combat. Arab philosophy is not specious. It is non fallacious. It is based on pure reasoning and logic. The Arabs I observed were military soldiers, the majority were non academic and many could neither read nor write. Nevertheless, apart from a few specifically appointed thoughtless guards, they reasoned with a high intelligence.

The Spahis cavalry soldiers, who captured us in the desert, were prime examples of men of high intelligence with great understanding and reasoning.

The Arab soldiers in the camp observed the prisoners with commendable discretion and were not insensitive to the pitfalls that awaited us in the desert when we escaped. They ostensibly disregarded our many acts of stupid behaviour in the camp, yet when things went wrong in consequence, they never adopted an 'I could have told you so' attitude. It would be acceptable to those unable to read the Koran for its teachings to be the word of God as dictated to Muhammad. I would have been reluctant to enter into serious competitive discussion or argument with an Arab scholar.

The military Arabs, to whom I spoke after our tunnel escape in the desert, pointed out unassumingly our short-sightedness and lack of wisdom. We had overlooked the possibility of encountering the nomadic bandits, who would not have hesitated to cut off a finger or fingers wearing gold rings. Painful removal of any gold filled teeth would have been routine.

• • • • • •

Prior to appel on Sunday mornings, the French officers and sous-officiers appeared before the parade dressed in their best uniforms, called by us their 'ponce' uniforms. The trousers were very wide with broad stripes down the sides. Our captors' appearance on these occasions encouraged us to practise using our vocal cords and to the tune of the song 'Bless 'em All' we would chant in unison as they stood before us,

"Here they are
In their f***ing great trousers with stripes down the sides,
With f***ing great pockets and f*** all inside
To the bastards we're saying 'goodbye'." Etc.

Then we would change the words and sing to another familiar tune,

"This is our story, this is our song,
We've been in Laghouat too f****ing long,
So roll on the Rodney, the Nelson, the Hood,
For this f***ing prison camp is no f***ing good!"

(Regrettably the Hood was sunk on 24th May 1941 in action against the Bismarck.)

In some respects, although our singing might have appeared to be pointless, it acted as a form of relief, we got something off our chests and our captors were left under no illusions regarding our feelings towards them.

• • • • • •

Petty Officer Wines, Fleet Air Arm Pilot back behind the wire under armed guard surveillance

HELLISH CONDITIONS

During the entire period of imprisonment Tony had written to his girlfriend Heather and in return he received regular comforting letters. For some months, however, she had not been well but bore her illness bravely and remained faithful to him throughout. As she never complained, Tony did not imagine her illness to be serious and looked forward to the day of his repatriation and return to England, when they hoped to get married. Tragedy struck when he received a letter from England, addressed in a handwriting he did not recognise. Hastily he tore open the envelope to read the dreadful contents, which informed him Heather had died after a short brave fight against insuperable odds. Still grasping the letter, Tony paced up and down the room, beating the wall with tightly clenched fists his distress almost turned to rage, "Why, oh why, does it happen to me? Why do women die on me?" he shouted.

I was lost for suitable words of consolation. Only the passing of time would help him now.

He faced up well to his sorrow and entered more wholeheartedly than ever into his editorial responsibilities towards The Camp Echo. Later, after careful preparation, he delivered two excellent lectures and creditably regained composure in spite of the trying elements of prison life.

• • • • • •

The hellish conditions in Laghouat became compounded in mid-August with the arrival of half the ship's company of HMS cruiser Manchester, torpedoed in the Mediterranean. The number of prisoners doubled overnight to reach a total of a thousand, resulting in at least one hundred British prisoners being crowded into rooms originally intended to house only twenty-four Arab soldiers.

It will come as no surprise that frequently prisoners had been known to yell uncontrollably at the top of their voices, "LEMME OUT! LEMME OUT! LEMME OUT!"

The sanitation in the caserne was becoming disgustingly evil beyond belief. The stench in the rooms, the colonnade and the compound and of dirty human bodies had to be experienced to be understood. The threat of epidemic disease was a real concern, not only of the prisoners but also of the Vichy French. For one man, who provided invaluable medical services to prisoners in the caserne, as described briefly in later pages, it was a situation of indescribable graveness.

He was Surgeon Lieutenant Robert Davies Royds M.B., Ch.B. (St.Andrews) Carnegie Research Scholar. As a Royal Naval Volunteer Reserve he served with HMS Havock. Tragically he died from polio at the age of 28 on 25th September 1942 and is commemorated at DELY IBRAHIM WAR CEMETERY Algeria. His home was in Scunthorpe, Lincolnshire.

The above information came from the Commonwealth War Graves Commission Certificate.

By this time the Royal Naval officers had taken over entirely the running of the camp, which the aircrew chaps now, called 'HMS Laghouat', the ship that ran aground in the Sahara! The Royal Navy was the senior service and let us know it. A petty officer was always regarded as senior to an RAF sergeant, a chief petty officer senior to a flight sergeant, whilst a midshipman was senior to a pilot officer and so on up the ranking scale.

We pleaded with our senior officers for RAF personnel to be allowed to run our own affairs, but in vain. It would not be possible. There was a possibility however, of the French transferring the RAF prisoners to an open camp at El Golea two hundred miles south, a possibility we welcomed, which never materialized.

With the kind permission of Mr John Whithouse from Seaton in Devon, I quote edited extracts from a précis article, part of a longer story he wrote about the late Commander Burfield, who had served as HMS Havock's First Lieutenant in 1942 and became a prisoner in Laghouat.

"Butlins and Laghouat did share one thing in common, in that they were Open to All Comers, officers, ratings, Swordfish pilots, Royal Air Force aircrew, Army personnel, big ships, small ships – all ranks from all Services, none were made welcome at Laghouat.

Before the arrival of 'Havock' the population was relatively small and the inmates looked after themselves on a somewhat casual basis. With 'Havock', however, there came a more recognisable routine. Cdr Jessel now became the Senior British Officer and a disciplined hierarchy was established which lasted until the position of SBO passed to Capt Drew RN, who had commanded the 'Manchester'.

There were the crews of two MTBs who entered Tunis under the mistaken impression that France was neutral and that they would be afforded the usual courtesy of 24 hours in which to effect repairs. They were of the opinion that they would have had a more civilised reception if they had sailed into Hamburg. The same fate had overtaken Captain Montgomery who had lost touch with his regiment at Dunkirk and had 'successfully' made his way to Algiers, only to find that he had made the same mistake as those off the MTBs.

A mixed bag indeed. Shot down pilots were common, mostly from Malta. Then there were the soldiers in addition to Captain Montgomery. There was Captain Adolph Cooper, a veteran of WWI, an ex Foreign Legion Sergeant, a baiter of the Vichy French, something of a nuisance sometimes, something of a mystery at all times and one of the genuine characters or eccentrics, which every community gathers to itself, in fact an 'adventurer', and whether his stories were true or not he gave an entertaining lecture.

No account of Laghouat would be complete without mention of the 'Manchesters'.

HMS Manchester was torpedoed off Cap Bon on 13th August, 1942, with the loss of over 150 lives. (I refer to a telephone quote on 14.01.04. from Mr Allan Walker now living in Saxilby, Lincolnshire, an ex Manchester crew member, who stated "with the loss of 12 lives.") The damage was contained for a while but eventually it was assumed that she could not be saved and the order was given to abandon ship. Another 150-odd men were rescued by the escorting destroyers."

Most of the captured crew of 'Manchester' reached Laghouat a week later, by which time almost a thousand men found themselves behind barbed wire in its fortified caserne.

At a later date one sailor discovered an Arab's cure for diarrhoea. This was to dry the outer skin of a pomegranate until it became hard, then using a stone, pound it to a powder and soak in water. According to the sailor the cure must have been successful. After twenty-four hours he became constipated!

This is a time to indulge in a little philosophical introspection. It should not be difficult to reflect less critically on adversity and seek more rewarding attributes, such as the characteristic qualities ascribed to persons. Contemplate their positive and generous contributions from which, at some time or other, we had all benefited during imprisonment. Must we always dwell on man's inhumanity to fellow man?

Let us consider all the camp activities, the splendidly organised camp concerts, boxing tournaments, gymnastic displays, lectures and debates, the library with its dog-eared books, supervised by willing enthusiasts. All these helped lighten the burden of inactivity, the malaise that breeds ennui and lassitude, the destroyer of a man's spirit, and his determination to withstand the trials with which he is beset.

During the earlier days at Laghouat, as mentioned already, I enjoyed typing the texts for The Camp Echo until moving into crowded living conditions following the arrival of the Havock crew and others. I then found it insupportable to carry on with this previously enjoyable occupation. Instead, I established two small classes that I was able to run in the colonnade, which provided space and was relatively free from interruptions. In one class I taught elementary French, i.e. basic grammar and simple conversation, about O level standard. In the other I talked on the basics of air navigation. By good fortune I had managed to retain my 1938 AP1234 Manual of Instruction that included the following pages of fifty-eight definitions. Sadly, somebody 'borrowed' the book, which they failed to return. It was found ultimately, dog-eared, dirty and torn in the remote filthy corner of a room. This angered me as the book was in excellent clean condition before it 'disappeared'. I never used it again.

One ordinary seaman, who was a schoolmaster, set exam papers to grade prisoners and the RAF boys came out top. Interesting lectures, delivered by prisoners well versed in their subjects, varied from banking and finance, accountancy, the British Press, parliamentary affairs, plumbing, the theatre and life in a circus to poaching. An army private, an escapee from Dunkirk, delivered the last talk. He had relied on his subject, poaching, to augment regular income in Civvy Street. I suppose it could be said that in this field he was an accomplished professional. Bill's talk was delivered simply and graphically. We all accompanied him as we evaded the gamekeeper, sometimes on the moors, sometimes wading in fast flowing rivers or walking along their banks seeking evasive plump trout and salmon. It was simpler snaring rabbits and trapping the almost defenceless pheasants. Bill may have been an adept provider for his family at home but he could do little in Laghouat to appease our hunger.

• • • • • •

On 2nd November 1942, Sergeant Gibbins, our camp postman wrote a letter to my parents, which he thought I might like to read before posting. It was a lovely, thoughtful letter, extracts from which I quote,

"I pull Doug's leg quite a bit about his letters, I do believe he really thinks I read them at times, he at any rate never seems to get worried about it, I often wonder if he ever worries about anything, he always has a smile on his face, no matter how black things look, and, they look pretty black at times. I am sure you have no need to worry about him, he is a picture of health and his 'they won't get me down' attitude will bring him out OK.

Most men are quite well, I am looking forward to the day of our freedom, and feel sure it is not so very far off now.

P.S. Have you found him a nice girl pen friend yet? Can you find me one?"

I read the letter, smiled and told him to send it off; it would buck up my folks no end.

Ironically, so shortly afterwards, remarkable news suddenly came from out of the blue. Early on Sunday morning 8th November 1942, we heard on our camp radio that the Allies had landed in North Africa and Algiers had surrendered. This turned out to be quite true but the Vichy French in Laghouat were disbelieving and at first could not be convinced. Their telephone lines from Algiers had been cut and they had no confirmatory knowledge of the landings having taken place.

Meetings were arranged hastily between the Foreign Legion Colonel, alias 'The Slug', and our senior British officers, meetings that we were not privy to attend. I understand that the very frightened Foreign Legion Colonel made some absurd proposals that were turned down. He was not only fearful now of the Arab guards, who really hated the French officers, but also of the British and Americans. He was in a no win situation, the biter was about to be bitten.

It was the concern of many of us that our captors may try and transfer us to Germany before the allies reached Laghouat. This did not arise, but in our pent up states of mind, we apprehensively feared the worst, anything was conceivable after our experiences during captivity. A transfer would have been extremely dangerous and the loss of lives under such circumstances would have been high. In spite of being unarmed, resistance could not have been ruled out. Unarmed prisoners defying armed guards of our Vichy French captors was a recipe for massacre.

This is what did happen:-

• • • • • •

I don't know how the situation became finally resolved between the British CO and the Vichy French, but I do know that a few days later, other old time prisoners and I were on the first lorry to head north for Djelfa.

It must be understood that prisoners, anxious to be released from the evil of Laghouat, included men from all over the world, including many from Australia, New Zealand, South Africa and Canada. There were different arrangements for the majority of Royal Navy personnel, in particular crews from destroyer Havock and cruiser Manchester.

My Canadian colleague Jim Templeton would be a prisoner to leave on one of the first lorries, but sadly he and I were split up on the journey back to England. Only recently I learned from his family in St. John's, Newfoundland, that Jim was taken to hospital in the UK before being sent home to Canada. His younger barrister son Ken explained that Jim was in rough shape when he returned home, due to malnutrition and ended up in hospital in Canada for a few months.

Some members of the Havock and Manchester crews held captive in Laghouat for only seven and three months respectively, experienced eating problems on repatriation. They suffered from jaundice, in some cases allegedly attributable to malnutrition. That news astonished me, but that is what I heard.

Surprisingly, I did not experience the feeling of elation I would have expected as the lorry moved out of the prison compound. My inside was numb. The change of events had occurred too quickly for comprehension. Could it be really true that those two and a quarter years of imprisonment were over and that I was on my way back to England to fly again in the war? Was I about to keep the promise I made in that letter to my relatives? I thought about Gibby's letter to my parents, posted on 2nd November, in which he said he was looking forward to the day of our freedom, and felt sure it was not so very far off. He must have been psychic! Would I arrive home before his letter reached my parents? I did, incredible as it may seem. I thought about the Vichy French officer, to whom I used to speak on the 'promenades' and his monosyllabic response to my question "pourquoi?" – "Prédestination".

Unbelievably, we were now travelling to freedom in the opposite direction over that arid inhospitable desert; the desert, which had caused us so much apprehension thirteen months earlier, in October 1941, during the unforgettable journey from Aumale.

• • • • • •

HOMEWARD BOUND

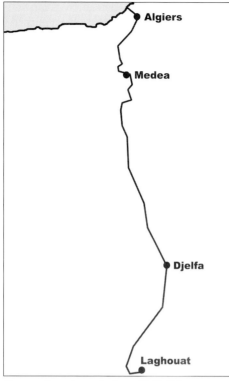

Homeward bound route, Laghouat-Djelfa-Algiers

This time on arrival at Djelfa we were taken quickly by train to a station outside Algiers. It had been a journey about which I have scant recollection. On arrival there was no loitering, we were marched immediately through narrow streets to the docks and taken on board HMS Keren, an old trading ship, now painted battleship grey and flying the White Ensign. It had landed American troops and rather than return with an empty hold was loaded with oranges, a scarcity and delicacy in the UK.

It was time now to climb out of the pit of hopelessness, polish up the navigator's slide rule and prepare to re-enter aerial combat against The Third Reich. Firstly, I had to get well and fit to resume flying.

A close friend of mine since schoolboy days, John Clayton, then a lieutenant in the Army, had landed in Algeria with the invasion forces. On making hasty enquiries, he learned that several British and Allied prisoners from Laghouat were aboard the Keren, scheduled to sail to the UK and that the ship's departure was imminent. Unfortunately an unexpected reunion, after a three years' separation, had been thwarted. Prior to the Keren sailing, John was moved with his regiment eastwards towards Tunis.

It was ironical that his involvement with North Africa should start as mine finished. Fortunately, he survived the ensuing campaigns and we became reunited two and a half years later. Our friendship still endures sixty-six years on.

We took our last look at the lights of Algiers before becoming enveloped in a smoke screen prior to sailing. It was then I heard the splash in the water some fifty feet below. Was a British stalwart about to keep his vow and 'get' that CO Vichy bastard from Aumale? I believe he was and I understand he did. "Vive l'esprit Anglais!" ("Long live the English spirit!")

I shed no tears next month, when I heard of the assassination of Admiral Darlan. Would it be too late now for the script writer to get busy amending "Oh! Vive de Gaulle?"

On board I had a very comfortable hospital bed, in which to relax throughout the journey home that took nearly a fortnight. The food was plentiful; more than my tired stomach could consume and of five stars standard compared with the rubbish we had consumed in North Africa. Although alcohol was available on board to all petty officers, when not on duty, it was strictly denied to all Royal Air Force aircrew senior NCOs, nor were we permitted the naval 'tot'.

Our ship docked at Gibraltar to refuel and we were allowed to go ashore for a few hours. It was on the Rock I bought a pair of fully-fashioned silk stockings, a present for mother and in the right size! After leaving Gibraltar the convoy sailed into stormy seas through the Bay of Biscay and continued in a westerly direction well out into the Atlantic to avoid the ever-present German U-boats. Fortunately I did not suffer from seasickness. When it was not dangerous to go forward on the open deck I would lean on the rail at the ship's bow and gaze at the mighty troughs. Close proximity to the ocean's powerful waters held no fear for me, as did the dark waters of the Mellégue. I felt safe on this ship and trusted that, when I resumed flying, my aircraft would never be forced to ditch.

We had been critical of the Royal Navy's attitude towards the RAF in Laghouat, but it was at a time like this I learned to appreciate the value of their services. The crews were not exposed to extreme danger for a few hours, as say the time of a bombing mission, but for weeks, sometimes months on end. We witnessed at first hand the incredible performances of the destroyers, whilst protecting the convoy and searching for enemy submarines. In the rough seas of the 'Bay' they would virtually disappear in the deep troughs then reappear and continue as if nothing had impeded them. The heroic sailors who manned them worked incessantly, whilst enduring the most cramped living conditions. I shall remain indebted to them all for their continued protection during the long voyage home.

The serenity of the scene we viewed, of ships in convoy sailing so placidly, belied the reality of this stage, which could so easily have become a watery grave. It represented a stage fraught with dangers, sometimes from the air, but always from the continual threats of invisible lurking German U-boats. The crews in those destroyers could not relax for a brief moment, evidenced by the almost ever-present flotsam.

We first sighted land off southern Ireland and shortly afterwards, on a grey late November day, anchored safely in the Firth of Clyde off Greenock.

After disembarking we parted company with the Royal Navy and Army personnel, the former being taken to Portsmouth. I have no idea what happened to the army boys. The RAF personnel were taken to Glasgow St Enoch's railway station and marched, under guard, to an awaiting train that was to take us overnight to London. Military guards remained with us throughout the journey and we were not allowed to make any contact with the public until we had been formally interrogated by senior RAF staff officers from the Air Ministry. Our imprisonment had ended but our freedom had not yet begun!

The following morning we were welcomed home by senior staff officers, mostly of air rank, who enquired about our treatment and asked our opinion of the Vichy French. Questions we had no difficulty in answering in depth. Then they asked did we think the Vichy French would be supportive of the allies now? Our response was on these lines. In late August 1940, when we needed their support it was not forthcoming, a situation that never changed during the entire time of our imprisonment. Now, with the unexpected change of events in North Africa, we were convinced they would support whichever side they thought would win.

My crew and I were then interviewed by a pompous Flight Lieutenant, who approached us carrying a large file of questionnaire papers. In an autocratic manner he was determined to 'throw the book' at us to learn why we had crashed a Blenheim on Cap Bon, Vichy French North Africa and not made the journey to Malta.

John Riddick, as captain of the Blenheim aircraft, was our spokesman and quick to interrupt the verbose flow of the questioner. He began by 'throwing the book' back at the Flight Lieutenant, who was left in no uncertainty where the blame originated. The hierarchy responsible for losing not just our Blenheim, but also for the loss that cost the lives of Pilot Officer D K Macdonald's crew, would find themselves in an extremely uncomfortable hot seat should groundless enquiries of an accusing nature be pursued. Without uttering a further word, the Flight Lieutenant closed his file and left the room, making his rapid tactful exit in complete contrition.

In the political arena the situation had become critical and it was explained to us how desperately Mr. Winston Churchill needed the backing of the entire French Nation. Retribution was understandable, but more important was the gaining of French co-operation. Restraint must be exercised, intimidation avoided and with a battle raging from Egypt westwards through Libya to the Tunisian frontier, we could not afford our relationship to become estranged. Mr. Churchill was sure we would understand.

So be it, or as we might have said in Laghouat, "entendu." Oh yes, we understood!

After the completion of interrogations, we were taken to stores and issued with new uniforms and other items of clothing. Later we collected leave passes, travel warrants and a handsome sum in back pay. Now freedom had begun!

Then I returned to the Endsleigh Hotel, where we had been billeted under guard during the last forty-eight hours, changed into my new uniform and prepared to return home. I was about to leave the hotel when I noticed my pilot, with his wife and colleagues, seated at a corner table near the bar. I went across to say farewell to a sick man. His charming wife knew she had welcomed home a husband, who was far from well, and most probably, whose service flying days were over. Sadness was written in her kind features, when I held her tiny hand and said goodbye. It was the last time I was to see either of them.

How more mistaken could I have been? John was certainly a sick man when I last saw him. From surprising information I received more than sixty-six years later on 28th June 2008, I learnt that John's health obviously improved. Shortly after repatriation, he was passed fit for operational flying again and joined 278 Air Sea Rescue Squadron. Sadly, whilst flying his CO's Tiger Moth to Denham on 12th May 1944, John was killed when the aircraft crashed. As my Blenheim pilot, he was one of the most experienced on 101 Squadron at West Raynham in July/August 1940. It is inconceivable he should die in a Tiger Moth.

Finally, I was really about to leave, when I noticed an RAF serviceman sitting alone at a far table with a glass in his hand. On the table were several empty bottles. Something had to be wrong. I recognised him at once, one of the old time prisoners, a married man and a tough flight sergeant navigator, referred to by some senior officers in the camp as a leader of men. He looked at me with tears in his eyes. "What's the matter?" I asked. Distress was written all over his face when he replied, "She's bloody left me." He hadn't even reached home and I learned afterwards his days of survival, after resumption of flying in Bomber Command, were to be numbered.

Feeling sad, I left the hotel on a miserable wet night and walked across to Euston Station to catch the night train for Manchester, where I would change trains and travel to my new home in Nelson. I had been unable to contact my parents, who were not aware I was even in the country; such had been the reticence of the authorities to broadcast news of our return. We had not been allowed to write pending clearance and my parents did not possess a telephone after moving from Manchester. New telephones for domestic purposes were not allowed.

As the train moved slowly out of the station, I realised that at last imprisonment was over. My thoughts turned to retribution. Yes, this had to come but not in the direction that caused Mr. Winston Churchill such concern.

The train reached Manchester's London Road Station at 04.00 hours and from here I had to walk across the city to Victoria Station to catch the milk train for Nelson. I had known the city streets like the back of my hand before the war, but now I was completely lost. Buildings that had been landmarks had disappeared and I witnessed in reality the destruction, about which we had heard in the prison camps. Sitting alone in the dimly lit railway carriage, on the last leg of the journey home, my mind was made up. Retribution it had to be.

The effect of two years' anxiety, fear and worry were visibly and inextricably etched on Mother's face, when she opened the door to welcome me home. It was a moment of emotion I shall not attempt to describe. Not until later in the day was I reunited with Father, in whose face I read a similar story. Never had I become more determined to do all in my power to inflict reprisals on those guilty of causing the suffering, which had been inflicted on my parents and on thousands of other completely defenceless civilians. If I had become weakened physically after more than

ENFIELD AIRMAN'S DEATH AND FUNERAL

SERGT.-AIR-GUNNER D. W. RANDALL

A FELLOW-OFFICER'S TRIBUTE

The "Gazette" regrets to record the death on Active Service of Sgt. Air-Gunner Douglas William Randall, of 58 The Sunny Road, Enfield.

'Aged 32, Sgt. Randall was for 2½ years an internee at Laghouat in Algeria, gaining his freedom in November, 1942, soon after which he was married.

In an interview with a "Gazette" reporter, a petty officer in the Royal Navy, who was in the same camp, spoke of the good work done by Sgt. Randall, who played a big part in the manning of the camps. He also produced a camp paper entitled the "Echo" and helped organise sports

in the camp. His final effort on behalf of the men who were held captive behind barbed wire, guarded by French native soldiers, was the part he played in organising an escape party.

Sgt. Randall joined the R.A.F. at the beginning of the war and had taken part in a number of operational flights over Germany.

two years of imprisonment, my resolution to seek revenge on the Nazi Germans was firm. This determination grew, when I walked along the London underground station platforms and witnessed the plight of the bombed out Londoners sleeping down there, huddled together in safety but in great discomfort as the trains thundered by.

At the beginning of October 1943 I received the tragic news concerning Tony Randall's death. After resuming operational flying, he had been killed when his Halifax bomber crashed near base returning from a raid over Germany. The tragedy was compounded by the fact that he had remarried shortly after repatriation.

THE ROAD BACK TO FLYING

After a period of eight weeks' rehabilitation leave, followed by two weeks for reselection at RAF Uxbridge, I failed to pass the aircrew medical test. In consequence, I was posted to Operational Training Unit (OTU) RAF Wymeswold near Loughborough, to carry out ground duties with Flying Control, as Air Traffic Control was called in those days.

I was to share a Nissen hut billet with four screened senior NCOs and benefit from the facilities of the Sergeants' Mess; a privilege denied to aircrew undergoing flying training. Most of the men patronising the bar were screened flying instructors, who had completed a tour of operational flights on the Vickers Wellington 'Wimpey' bomber. They were all strangers to me and I felt rather alone and somewhat apprehensive, when I asked if anyone played Bridge. Shades of Laghouat! The response delighted me and a Bridge school was formed immediately. For the next three months, before returning to flying, I enjoyed the 'born again' therapy with my new colleagues.

On duty with other grounded aircrew, I shared the responsibilities of Flying Control; working in the caravan off the runway, marshalling aircraft on take offs and landings. Between us we devised an unofficial strategy whereby we enjoyed the benefits of regular forty-eight hours off duty passes. With a little help from a kindly disposed young lady in the orderly room, we obtained a supply of undated leave passes. This omission we had no difficulty in rectifying when required. To enable the system to work satisfactorily, we created our own 'on duty rosters' often entailing unofficial long hours on.

I had completed a long stint on night duties by the morning of the 19th February 1943 and was free to go on forty-eight hours unofficial pass. Tired from lack of sleep, I was undecided whether to travel home or relax on base. A colleague told me that a vehicle was scheduled to leave the guardroom for Loughborough station, so if I hurried I could get a lift and catch the next train from London to Manchester. My mind was made up. I would travel home.

The train was crowded at Loughborough and I was fortunate to find a vacant seat in a Pullman carriage. Although I was aware of the attractive young lady on my right, I settled quickly and being tired, promptly fell asleep. At Sheffield station I became wide-awake and turned towards the young lady, who asked if the train was running late. I had no idea. It was not the question that attracted me but her lovely smile. We began to talk and became completely engrossed in conversation. The train arrived all too quickly, or so it seemed, at Manchester, where we crossed the city to Victoria station. Whilst waiting for our respective trains to Blackburn and Nelson, standing on a windy platform we hurriedly exchanged names and addresses. Afterwards we corresponded regularly and met whenever possible. This led to Alice Ormerod from Blackburn and I becoming engaged in June 1943, one year after the completion of the Laghouat escape tunnel and six months before I resumed operational flying.

Let me tell you now about her family.

• • • • • •

The town of Blackburn derived its name from the burn Blake, on the banks of which a few dwellings stood many hundreds of years ago. At the turn of the century the population exceeded 100,000, composed mostly of cotton mill workers living in crowded back streets near their respective mills. Blackburn lay in a densely populated bowl. The better quality properties were built on the West End hillside, leading towards Preston New Road, Revidge then on to Mellor. This could be described as the gateway to the most spectacular countryside North East and North West. It led to such areas as Longridge Fell, the Lake District, Forest of Bowland and Yorkshire Dales National Park and continued further north to the Scottish border.

Forebears of Thomas Ormerod, father of Isaac, (Alice's Grandfather) included one who was knighted for work he carried

Alice

out on Greenwich Observatory. Thomas was foreman stonemason on the building of Blackburn Town Hall Library, and was noted for carved illustrations of the trade and industry of the town.

The father of Elizabeth Haydock, wife of Isaac Ormerod, owned a traction engine in the days when a person was required to walk in front waving a red flag. His sister married Richard Slater and they emigrated to the USA. After staking a claim on a plot of land, of which they were robbed, they trekked by covered wagon through South and North Dakota to Gladman, Saskatchewan, where Richard opened his own coal mine. His son married a Red Indian girl and brought her to Blackburn. It created quite a stir and no little interest in the town, when she arrived, dressed in full Red Indian costume!

Isobel Duckworth, a forebear of Elizabeth wife of Gilbert Ormerod (Alice's father), was educated at a convent in France and married Joseph Francis Miller, Director of Education for Brighton and Hove. His brother was a Cardinal at the Vatican.

Isaac Ormerod was a prominent figure in Blackburn and with other businessmen was involved at the time of the founding of Blackburn Rovers Football Club, in which he became a

Alice

shareholder. This was before the club played its first League game in September 1888, after being invited to become a member of the newly formed Football League.

The club moved in 1890 to what is still its present site at Ewood Park.

Isaac married Elizabeth, daughter of John and Elizabeth Duckworth, whose marriage had been arranged by special

Isaac Ormerod (Circa 1905)

dispensation from the Pope, the Duckworths being a wealthy and influential catholic family.

He was a shrewd business man, the founder and Chairman of Directors of Cotton Brothers Co. Ltd. at Appleby Street Mill and later at Pump Street Mill in Blackburn. The responsibilities of running the mill were later assigned to his son Gilbert.

The St. John Ambulance Brigade in Blackburn owed much to the energetic leadership of Gilbert, who joined in 1908 and passed through the various NCO ranks in seven years to become officer in charge. On the outbreak of World War One he was one of the first men in uniform to leave Blackburn and qualified for duty to organise the running of a Field Military Hospital at Netley in Hampshire. Here, they received and tended wounded soldiers from the battlefields of France. Unfit for active service, Gilbert returned to Blackburn in 1915. Throughout the remainder of the war he assisted in training three hundred men for service with the medical units of the Army and Navy.

In recognition of valuable services rendered to the Order of St. John, he was appointed Honorary Serving Brother in 1920 and received the long-service medal in 1922. In 1924, he was commanded by the King to be present at a garden party at Buckingham Palace.

He went on to become a prominent Freemason, a member of United Brethren Lodge and the Knights Templar. He continued to carry out his mill duties with expertise as Chairman of Directors, until his untimely death in 1936 at the age of fifty-three. Gilbert's relationship and understanding with his loyal workers was beyond reproach and earned their highest respect. He was a man of great magnanimity, who made personal financial sacrifices in times of depression to ensure the mill did not face closure.

The relationship with his Leicester friend Thomas Cook, the travel agent, enabled him to hire a coach every year and finance a brief holiday in Holland for his workers, quite an unprecedented gesture in those days. (Thomas Cook's Leicester home is now the Leicestershire and Rutland Branch Headquarters of the British Red Cross).

Gilbert's proposal of marriage to Elizabeth Duckworth, whose family was strong Roman Catholic, presented problems. He was a Congregationalist and to enable the marriage to take place, Elizabeth renounced her catholic commitments. Their three daughters, Elizabeth, Evalyn and Alice, were encouraged to attend the local Church of England church. This was the nearby St. Silas Church on Preston New Road, Blackburn, where subsequently all three daughters were married.

Elizabeth was a devout and gentle lady, who outlived her husband by sixteen years. He never enjoyed robust health and uncomplainingly, she nursed him for several years before his death. She was a loving mother, wholeheartedly devoted to the interests and education of her three

Gilbert & Elizabeth Ormerod 1924 in Corporation Park Blackburn

Gilbert Ormerod in St John's uniform

daughters, on whom she lavished love and kindness, but not to the exclusion of correction and discipline, when required.

Before joining Blackburn High School, Alice the youngest, like her sisters, was sent to Cross Hill kindergarten at an early age. One day, she came home in great distress. "It's mi shoes," she kept saying. Her mother examined the footwear and could find nothing wrong. "No, no, it's mi shoes, it's mi shoes." This bewildered her. Alice would not normally pronounce my as 'mi'. Finally the problem was resolved. A new teacher had been appointed in the kindergarten, a Miss Hughes, who had been cross!

A pall of industrial smoke hung heavily over the Lancashire cotton mill towns during at least fifty working weeks of the year. For one week the mills closed for the annual wakes (holiday). The boilers were shut down for cleaning and de-scaling, the smoke pall disappeared and Lancashire folk, who were not on holiday, could breathe fresh air. During this one week, Gilbert obtained some relief from his chronic asthma. The only other place locally, where he could breathe more easily was on Pendle Hill. He was unable to climb on his own, so his daughters helped him with the aid of a rope.

Just over nineteen hundred feet in height, Pendle Hill dominates the countryside around for several miles. It lies to the North West of Nelson and the North East of Blackburn and from either town is easily discernible. Its huge flat backbone constitutes an unmistakable landmark.

To say that each chimney, towering like a proud smoking sentinel over its mill, was a thing of beauty, might be granting the author an unqualifiable descriptive licence. Collectively, however, the chimneys formed an eye-catching landscape, to be found, most probably, nowhere else in England other than the industrial north. To withstand the rigours of all weathers, expert maintenance was undertaken by highly trained steeplejacks. Their courage and expertise was incomparable, as they scaled the face of these bricks and mortar swaying giants, to establish scaffolding, which offered little protection hundreds of feet above the ground. In her childhood days, Alice watched these men in awe and admiration.

When Alice was beginning to spell and write, she had been asked at school to compose a short story. Gilbert, by now, was suffering with serious asthma. It was the accepted duty of his daughters to clean and polish his boots each morning, then take them to his bedroom before he dressed. In her story, Alice misspelt the word boots. The sentence read "I take Father's 'boos' to his bedroom." This caused a few wry smiles. He was a total abstainer.

Whilst learning to count at kindergarten, one of the children struggled to ten, faltered and stopped. "What follows ten?" the teacher asked the class. "Jack, queen, king," came Alice's quick response, to the teacher's astonishment. Alice had been taught to play Patience at an early age, so that she could play quietly on her own, while her father, who was unwell, was resting.

Gilbert was a devoted father. In spite of his asthma, the welfare and education of his daughters were always uppermost in his mind. When Alice showed an interest in music at an early age, he did not ignore a possible pianoforte potential. He was delighted, when as a birthday present, an aunt bought her an Adams baby grand piano. A modification was required to enable her to reach the pedals and after this had been carried out, Alice began to practise. Gilbert's expectations were to be realised. From a child embryo, a lifelong pianist was born.

When her father was unwell, or resting, Alice would always seek his permission before practising. He rarely refused and would lie in bed listening, enjoying and gauging her progress. The sounds of her playing were almost therapeutic, as though they engendered a feeling of well being and contentment. They were the forerunners of achievement.

The photograph of Elizabeth and Gilbert was taken in 1924 at Corporation Park, created about the 1860 period onwards, at a time when the cotton industry was depressed. To carry out this project, which led to a house building development of good quality properties towards the Preston New Road area, the Corporation found employment for out of work mill operatives. The park, ten minutes walk from Alice's home at Azalea Road, provided the family and local people with a quiet haven for relaxation. Its well cared for gardens, excellent collection of plants in the conservatory, tennis courts and bandstand provided splendid amenities.

Gilbert's responsibilities with the St. John Ambulance required his regular attendance at Ewood Park for Blackburn Rovers' home matches. Like his father Isaac, he was a shareholder in the club and was privileged to have a seat in the directors' box. The entire family were staunch supporters of the club, including a very young Alice. On match days she would stand at the gate of the house at Azalea Road and with the wind in the right direction, could hear the cheers from the crowd at the ground. She became adept at predicting the number of goals scored by Rovers and would await eagerly the paper boy to seek confirmation from the stop press news.

In April 1928, approaching the age of twelve, she watched intrigued, as a young man in a neighbour's backyard raised a bucket above his head. Pretending the bucket was the F. A. Cup; the young man turned and brandished it aloft as if to face an imaginary crowd. This was practice, in the hope that he might be required to lift the real thing. Who was this young man? He was Harry Healess, the Blackburn Rovers captain, whose aspirations became fulfilled, when on 21st April 1928, Blackburn Rovers beat Huddersfield Town by three goals to one in the F. A. Cup Final at Wembley. On retirement from football, Harry ran a newsagent's business at Limefield - a short walk from Azalea Road.

The Rovers team sheet for the 1928 Final read:-

Campbell, Rankin, Crawford, Hutton, Jones, Thornewell, Puddefoot, Roscamp, Healess, McLean, Rigby.

Douglas Shorrock was born in 1923, quite near to Alice's home, in Azalea Road, Blackburn. He attended St. Silas' Elementary School, at the back of Azalea Road, and later Queen Elizabeth's Grammar School. In 1933 his father enrolled him as a member of East Lancs Cricket Club, whose home was Alexandra Meadows. At this time, Gilbert Ormerod was a member of the club and took his youngest daughter Alice to watch many of the home games, played in this beautiful setting. Neither Douglas Shorrock, nor Alice Ormerod, imagined that seventy years later they would become closely acquainted. Douglas discovered in 2003 that my wife came from Blackburn. Later in correspondence, Alice mentioned that the game, which attracted the largest crowd at the Meadows was against Nelson, for whom the West Indian lawyer Leary Constantine played. He was a highly respected professional and probably the most accomplished slip fielder in the league.

In 1934 Gilbert Ormerod bought a Citroën car, in which his three daughters learned to drive. It was used as a family car, primarily for their father's benefit, to enable him to travel in comfort and avoid the smoky atmosphere of public transport. In January 1935 Alice received her full driving licence issued by Blackburn County Borough Council.

Four years earlier, Gilbert Ormerod had retired as Superintendent of the St. John Ambulance Brigade, a position he held for thirteen years. He was a public figure in Blackburn, held in high esteem for the services he rendered to the community. As mentioned earlier he was completely teetotal, that was until the day before he died. An anomalous situation was reached, when seriously ill in bed, he asked for a piece of Christmas cake and a glass of champagne. To the surprise of those present, he partook of this refreshment and died a few hours later.

A public funeral took place in early January 1936. It was an impressive ceremony. The 'LAST POST' and 'REVEILLE' were played at the graveside.

His cap, belt and ambulance decorations, resting on a black

velvet cushion, and the Ambulance Corps Flag, were placed on the coffin. A detachment of the Ambulance Brigade marched with the cortège, which included two open cars laden with flowers. The streets on the funeral route were lined with police and members of the St. John Ambulance Association Brigade. Masonic representatives attended and citizens turned out in large numbers to join them to pay their last respects at the passing of a loved friend.

For Elizabeth his widow, and her three daughters, Elizabeth, Evalyn and Alice, it was an unforgettable emotional experience.

After the funeral, a reporter said, "He died as he had lived, with everything in order. I can honestly say, I knew a man."

Alice continued as a student teacher of music at Blackburn High School for girls, where she had been educated. A friend and contemporary of her sister Evalyn, was Kathleen Ferrier, who became internationally famous as a singer with a deep contralto voice. Although Kathleen was four years older than Alice, their mutual interest in piano playing resulted in the development of a close association. Sadly Kathleen died of cancer in 1953 at the age of forty-one. One of her most popular songs 'Blow the Wind Southerly' was Alice's well remembered favourite, played movingly, at her own funeral.

At the age of twenty-one Alice left the High School to attend the Royal Academy of Music in London, where she gained two diplomas and became Alice Ormerod LRAM ARCM.

She was appointed specialist teacher of pianoforte and elocution at the Prebendal High School for girls in Aylesbury, Buckinghamshire, where she taught throughout the Second World War. In the junior department of the school there were facilities for the tuition of little boys. One of these youngsters, to whom she taught elocution and music, was to become a well known personality in broadcasting. He was Richard Dimbleby's son David.

• • • • • •

I arrived with my crew on New Year's Eve 1943 at 100 Lancaster Squadron Waltham near Grimsby. Ten days later we received a brand new Avro Lancaster heavy bomber HW-R and carried out our first operational flight on 14th January 1944 to Brunswick in Germany.

Our tour of thirty operational sorties was completed on 7th June 1944 the day after the D Day Landings. It included three raids incurring Bomber Command's greatest losses of heavy bombers during the war, namely: -

19/20 February	1944	79 aircraft	Leipzig
24/25 March	1944	73 aircraft	Berlin
30/31 March	1944	97 aircraft	Nurnberg

During this period Bomber Command lost over one thousand five hundred heavy bombers, accounting for the loss of over ten thousand five hundred aircrew.

I mentioned that when we joined 100 Squadron, my fiancée started to keep an independent small diary, in which little book she recorded brief details of the targets and losses during operational flights carried out by Bomber Command. I am now reading from its faded pages. These are extracts after we completed our operational tour.

1944

Jan 14	Brunswick	38 missing	1
Jan 20	Berlin	35 missing	2
Feb 15	Berlin	43 missing	3
Feb 19	Leipzig	79 missing	4
Feb 20	Stuttgart	10 missing	5
Feb 24	Schweinfurt	35 missing	6
Feb 25	Augsburg	24 missing	7
March 1	Stuttgart	4 missing	8
March 15	Stuttgart	37 missing	9

No record for number 10

March 18	Frankfurt	22 missing	11
March 22	Frankfurt	33 missing	12
March 24	Berlin	73 missing	13
March 25	Essen	9 missing	14
March 30	Nuremberg	94 missing	15
April 9	Minelaying	11 missing	16
April 10	Railway Targets	22 missing	17
April 18	various targets	14 missing	18
April 20	Cologne	16 missing	19
April 22	Dusseldorf	42 missing	20
May 10	France	15 missing	21
May 12	Sea mining	14 missing	22
May 21	Duisburg	30 missing	23
May 22	Dortmund	35 missing	24
May 24	Dieppe	28 missing	25
May 27	Merville	27 missing	26
May 31	Tergnier	8 missing	27
June 2	Dieppe Beneval	17 missing	28
June 5	Crisbecq	losses not recorded	29
	Targets coast of France		
June 6	Battle area	13 missing	30

In addition to operational flying on 100 Squadron, I carried out nine instructional missions tutoring Lancaster operational navigators on the use of the radar aid H2S. The pilots of all aircraft were as listed below.

09.02.44	Lancaster 111 S	Fg Off Hamilton	Initial Demonstration
10.02.44	"	Flt Lt Ross	" " "
23.02.44	" T	Fg Off Sherriff	" " "
03.03.44	"	W/O Cook	" " "
01.04.44	" B	Flt Lt Innes	Pass out check
08.05.44	" G	Flt Lt Eames	" " "
14.05.44	" Q	Sqn Ldr Hamilton	" " "
26.05.44	" U	Plt Off Smith	" " "
29.05.44	" U	Plt Off Mills	" " "

After completion of the tour, I flew thirty-eight hazardous instructional missions on less reliable aircraft (eighteen Halifax and twenty Lancaster) with navigators whose pilots were inexperienced on four engine bombers and less reliable aircraft. These were at Conversion Units, one of which Sandtoft irreverently earned the pseudonym "Prangtoft".

Conversion Unit 1662 Blyton

Date	Aircraft	Pilot	Notes
10.07.44	Halifax 111 K2	Sgt Sutton	X Country
12.07.44	" M	Plt Off Trent	Duty not completed
15.07.44	" M	Plt Off Trent	X Country

Conversion Unit 1667 Sandtoft

Date	Aircraft	Pilot	Notes		
13.09.44	Halifax N	Flt. Lt. Young	Initial Dem/X Country		
14.09.44	" N	Flt. Lt. Murton	"	"	"
21.09.44	" W	Fg Off Purves	"	"	N.C.O.
23.09.44	" W	Fg Off Purves	"	"	N.C.O.
25.09.44	" Z	Fg Off Eames	"	"	N.C.O.
26.09.44	" N	Plt Off Hanna	"	"	/X Country
04.10.44	" V	Plt Off Walters	"	"	"
09.10.44	" C2	Plt Off Jolly	"	"	"
10.11.44	" M2	Fg Off Matkin	"	"	"
22.10.44	" G	Plt Off Smithers	"	"	"
26.10.44	" G	Plt Off Black	"	"	"
04.11.44	" D	Fg Off Ayres	"	"	"
16.11.44	" E2	Fg Off Wilson	"	"	"
19.11.44	" V	Plt Off Wannop	"	"	"
21.11.44	" P2	Flt Lt Hughes	"	"	"
04.01.45	Lancaster M	W/O Howlett	"	"	"
06.01.45	" F	Fg Off Mc.Larty	"	"	"
12.01.45	" Y	Flt Sgt Wilson	"	"	"
16.01.45	" Z	Flt Sgt Hilder	"	"	"
20.01.45	" P	Plt Off Kelly	"	"	"
03.02.45	" F	Plt Off Sear	"	"	"
04.02.45	" Z	Fg Off Martin	"	"	"
05.02.45	" T	Flt Sgt Darmody	"	"	"
09.02.45	" E	Flt Sgt Abercrombie	"	"	"

09.02.45	"	E	Flt Sgt Abercrombie	"	"	"
10.02.45	"	P	Flt Sgt Ryans	"	"	"
22.02.45	"	Z	Plt Off Bramble	"	"	"
24.02.45	"	H	Flt Sgt Richmond	"	"	"
25.02.45	"	D	Flt Sgt Richmond	"	"	"
05.03.45	"	D	Flt Sgt Tandy	"	"	"
07.03.45	"	P	Flt Sgt Roberts	"	"	"
12.03.45	"	M	W/O Lough	"	"	"
16.03.45	"	L	Sgt Graham	"	"	"
20.03.45	"	H	Plt Off Morgan	"	"	"
					N.C.O.	
21.03.45	"	E	Plt Off Morgan	"	"	"

FINIS

The losses reported on some of the later French targets include those incurred on other targets in that area by Bomber Command aircraft.

Extract from the diary which Alice kept and to which I refer in the text. Between 18/19th March to 30/31st March 1944

* * * * * *

On 19th June 1945 and 20th July 1945 I flew as navigator over Dutch and German territories in Mark III Lancasters piloted by Flight Lieutenant Atkinson and Flight Lieutenant Des Sargent DFC. We carried an attractive payload of Waafs on sightseeing missions at 2,000 feet over fifteen devastated cities, two regrettably Dutch, namely Arnhem and Rotterdam. The other thirteen were cities of the German Reich. Photographs on accompanying pages illustrate some of the areas of devastation.

3   Emden

15   Wilhelmshaven

1945
Note the sunken
ship

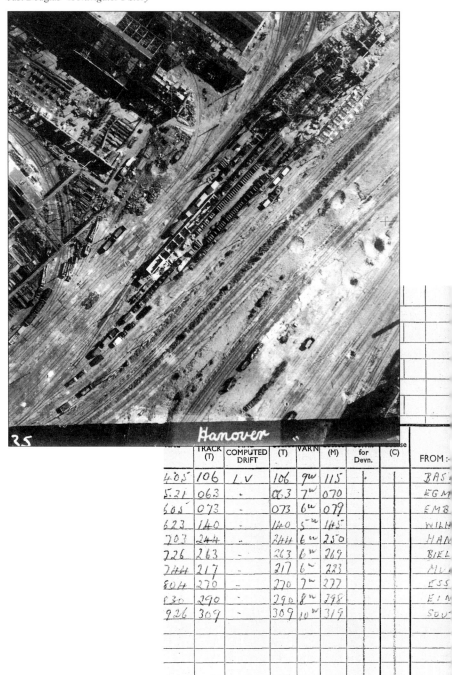

TIME	TRACK (T)	COMPUTED DRIFT	(T)	VARN	(M)	for Devn.	(C)	FROM :-
405	106	1 V	106	9ʷ	115	.		BAS
5.21	063	.	063	7ʷ	070			EGM
605	073	-	073	6ᵘ	079			EMB
623	140	-	140	5ᵘ	145			WILH
703	244	-	244	6ᵘ	250			HAN
726	263	-	263	6ʷ	269			BIEL
744	217	-	217	6ᵘ	223			ML
804	270	-	270	7ᵘ	277			ESS
830	290	-	290	8ᵘ	298			EIN
926	309	-	309	10ᵘ	319			SOU

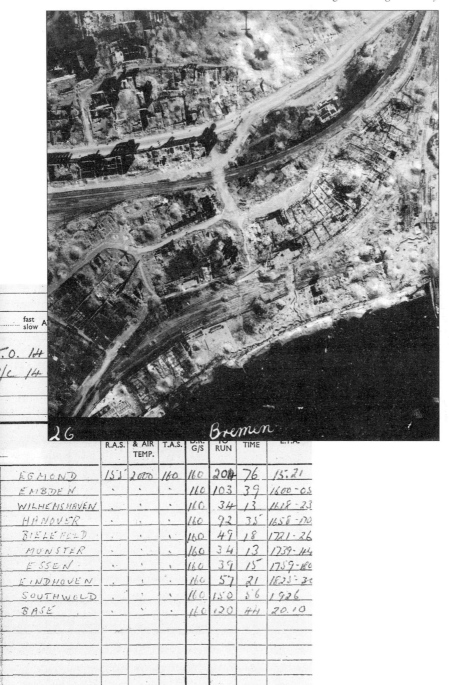

	R.A.S.	& AIR TEMP.	T.A.S.	D.R. G/S	TO RUN	TIME	E.T.A.
EGMOND	155	2000	160	160	204	76	15.21
EMBDEN	"	"	"	110	103	39	1600-05
WILHEMSHAVEN	"	"	"	160	34	13	1618-23
HANOVER	"	"	"	160	92	35	1658-170
BIELEFELD	"	"	"	160	49	18	1721-26
MUNSTER	"	"	"	160	34	13	1739-44
ESSEN	"	"	"	160	39	15	1759-180
EINDHOVEN	"	"	"	160	57	21	1825-30
SOUTHWOLD	"	"	"	160	150	56	1926
BASE	"	"	"	160	120	44	20.10

RÉSUMÉ BY THE AUTHOR

My operational tour on the Avro Lancaster HW-R from 100 Squadron at Waltham, finished on the morning of 7th June 1944. The Station Medical Officer Sqn Ldr 'Doc' Marshall would not allow us to continue flying without a rest from operational sorties.

I met my first four crew members at Wymeswold Operational Training Unit (OTU), who were later to join two others and complete my Lancaster crew. It was then I made one point quite clear to them, "I spent two and a quarter years in three prisoner of war camps and have no intention of this happening again. When you are not flying, what you do in your spare time is within reason your affair. What you do when you fly with me is very much my affair."

After completion of our tour, I was delighted to pay them all the highest tributes. They had been the most supportive and brave men with whom any aircrew could wish to fly. They had been outstanding in every department. To a man, in spite of knowing the dangers involved, they always climbed on board our aircraft fearless but determined to take the war to the Nazis. This is exactly what they did.

THERE IS NO 'I' IN TEAM. Six aircrew were the men who flew with me on operational sorties. The groundcrew were the men and women, without whose tireless support, our Lancaster bomber could not have flown. Both crews relied upon cooperation from all other members of the operational station.

As I write this text in my ninety-fourth year, I am rewarded by the increasing awareness, particularly by the younger generation, of the sacrifices made by all those people who served when helping their country withstand and combat the dangers, hazards and horrors of Naziism.

More awareness should be forthcoming regarding the behaviour of the Vichy French during WW2. In the pages of this book I have not been hesitant in expressing my feelings towards them. In this context I quote an extract from a letter sent to me by a reader in Dunfermline of my earlier books.

"My mother was friendly with a French woman from Calais who had been arrested a number of times by the Boche for childish acts of mischief and bore the scars of her interrogator's dagger on her legs, as he tried to get Jaquie to confess to being a 'maquisard'. Jaquie said when I asked her what she thought of the Germans, "I can forgive but not forget." But at the mention of the Vichy French her rage was literally volcanic and it was almost frightening being in the same room. I think she hated them more than she did the Germans..."

I wish to extend my appreciative thanks to the three ladies who contributed so warmly in the Prefaces of 'Just Douglas'.

Sandra is my supportive friend, helpful influence and neighbour.

Fortuitously, I met Marguerite and Lola during my book signings at The Battle of Britain Memorial Flight, RAF Coningsby and The Lincolnshire Aviation Heritage Centre, East Kirkby.

I am privileged to be closely associated with the undermentioned. This substantiates my earlier comments regarding increasing awareness.

The Trent Wing ATC and Cadets covering Derbyshire, Nottinghamshire and Lincolnshire.

Worksop College, Woodard Schools (Nottinghamshire) Ltd

William Farr (Church of England) Comprehensive School, Dunholme Lodge, Lincolnshire. (Former site of RAF Dunhome Lodge, home of 44 Rhodesia Squadron, 49, 170, and 619 Squadrons during World War 2.)

Worksop College
Worksop
Nottinghamshire S80 3AP
Telephone: 01909 537127
Fax: 01909 537102

email: headmaster@worksopcollege.notts.sch.uk
www.worksopcollege.notts.sch.uk

Mr. R. A. Collard M.A., Headmaster

12th November 2009

Mr. J.D. Hudson,
1 Sheppard's Close,
Heighington,
LINCOLN,
LN4 1TU

Dear Mr. Hudson,

Thank you so much for your letter. It is very good of you to write.

I can assure you that we were enormously touched by your presence on Sunday evening. Many parents and pupils have mentioned it to me since and I know that several of them spoke to you during the evening. I was especially moved by the heartfelt way in which you proclaimed the sentence of remembrance. I shall not forget that for a very long time.

You know that you are always welcome at the College. You have won a place in the affection of many people here. Members of the Lower Sixth yesterday took Assembly and, as it was Armistice Day, they dedicated their talk to Harry Patch and Henry Allingham.

We wish you well and look forward to seeing you again at the College.

With best wishes.

Yours sincerely,

Woodard Schools (Nottinghamshire) Limited: a company registered in England and Wales. Company Number 5011039.
Registered Office: Worksop College, Worksop, Nottinghamshire S80 3AP. Registered Charity Number 1103326.

William Farr - Church of England Comprehensive School
Unveilling of the Memorial Window, RAF Dunholme Lodge 1942-1945, Sunday 12th July 2009
By J Douglas Hudson DFC AE RAFVR

The young professional photographer is an ex scholar of William Farr School

EXTRACT FROM
DIARY OF 100 SQUADRON WALTHAM'S
LANCASTER 'R Roger' FOR MARCH 1944.

1/2	March	Stuttgart
15/16	March	Stuttgart
18/19	March	Frankfurt
22/23	March	Frankfurt
24/25	March	Berlin
25/26	March	Essen
30/31	March	Nuremberg

30th March 2004 marked the sixtieth anniversary of the disastrous Nuremberg raid by the RAF, when Bomber Command lost ninety-seven heavy bombers. The attached picture, taken at the East Kirkby Lincolnshire Aviation Heritage Centre, speaks for itself. It appears by 'Courtesy of the Lincolnshire Echo' and also by kind permission of Mr Fred and Mr Harold Panton.

Alice and I were married on 24th March 1945 in the Church of England Church, St. Silas Church, Blackburn.

Alice was courteous, unassuming, deeply intelligent, of profound learning, yet never pretentious. Her radiant natural smile was of aesthetic beauty. It was her hallmark to be remembered always.

She was a little lady with great strength of character. Her deep

Christian faith gave her a great understanding and tolerance to combat problems. Her greatest contribution to life was the impeccable manner in which she brought up, and with much wisdom, assured the good education and welfare of our two daughters, who are her priceless legacy.

Douglas and Alice's Wedding

PRICELESS LEGACIES

*Ann feeding
Yvonne at Cheadle
Hulme in 1950*

Alice and Ann at the front gate Cheadle Hulme

Grannie Ormerod and Ann at Cheadle Hulme

Alice and Yvonne on lawn Cheadle Hulme

Yvonne standing

Ann at fence with Nicholas, the little boy from next door at Cheadle Hulme

Alice's priceless legacy children at Cheadle Hulme (above left) Yvonne and (above right) Ann

Yvonne

Yvonne

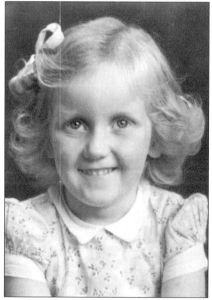

Ann

*Enid
Brimelow
with Ann
at Cheadle
Hulme*

Highclere and lily pond Four Oaks

Highclere Garden

Highclere Garden, 2 on the swing, the collie dog, Yvonne in the rockery and Ann on a tricycle on the back lawn

THE AFTERMATH

The following comments from Ken Templeton in St. John's Newfoundland revealed that his father Jim had had similar experiences. "Since he had had 29 missions over France and Germany from Jan 1941 to June, when he was shot down (by Royal Navy action!), he was put back into Bomber Command. He was sent to Pat Bay, British Columbia, to train Canadians in aerial gunnery. Dad often said the experiences he had with rookie pilots were in many ways more hair-raising than flying over Bremen, Cologne or Berlin.

On becoming his father's lawyer in pension litigation in 1985, Ken tackled the bureaucrats when it was said the Allies may have been at war with Vichy but there was no instance where the French were at war with the Allies." (Points I state in the early pages of this book). Ken goes on to say, "The Crown caved in and gave all the claimants their pensions retroactively and it includes a widow's benefit, I believe there is an equivalent pension in the UK, you should check it out."

I did, and sadly there is not. I approached two authorities. Each authority referred me to the other. Neither had ever heard of Vichy French North African prisoner of war camps.

If there were such a pension, it would provide a very splendid windfall to help combat frailties in my ninety-fourth year. I could then afford to pay for carers.

It was rewarding to hear from Ken after he had read my book, 'There and Back Again - A NAVIGATOR'S STORY'. He stated how the uncertainty of the length of confinement in the filth and close quarters of Laghouat must have been unbearable at times "Thank you for encouraging each other to survive. I am sure my Dad wouldn't have lived through it without friends like you."

I would say it was unbearable all the time. We would en ask each other the question, was it better to live with the ertainty of not knowing the length of confinement? There were divided opinions on this. I believed it was better not to know; better to hope and anticipate.

After repatriation it was inevitable the axe would fall in certain directions. In this context it fell on Lieutenant Commander Watkins, Captain of destroyer HMS Havock and Captain Drew, Captain of cruiser HMS Manchester. Both naval officers were court-martialled and relieved of their commands. The action of Captain Drew in authorising his ship to be scuttled, certainly saved the lives of nearly one thousand men, about five hundred of whom became prisoners of war in Laghouat. The others were ferried to Gibraltar.

For Commander R F Jessel ex Captain of HMS Legion, the story of success continued. He pursued his wartime service career with distinction to become Commander RN OBE DSO DSC and Bar and three times Mentioned in Despatches.

In the Supplement to THE LONDON GAZETTE of Tuesday the 5th January 1943 Signalman E S (Ted) Clayton was mentioned in recognition of gallant and distinguished services in the field.

Gunner Leslie Harold (Daffy) Watson Royal Horse Artillery and Gunner Frederick Harry Williams Royal Horse Artillery were both mentioned for their awards of The Military Medal in recognition of similar gallant and distinguished services.

After demobilisation in early 1946, I put all matters relating to my experiences during World War Two completely out of mind. I did not discuss the Second World War, make any attempt to attend reunions, join any RAF associations or re-contact wartime contemporaries.

This was to change fifty-four years later. Doug Chapman my bomb aimer introduced me to Nick and Carol Carter, who were compiling a Register listing recipients of The Distinguished Flying Cross from its inception in 1918 as far as 1995. Intrigued by my wartime experiences as a prisoner of war in Vichy French North

Africa and how survival led ultimately to my return to operational flying, they persuaded me to write a book in an attempt to fill a gap in history. In consequence, my book 'There and Back Again – A NAVIGATOR'S STORY' was born in the year 2001.

My wife Alice supported me over fifty-nine years of married life and left the legacy of two daughters, when she died tragically on 30th May 2004, the year leading to our Diamond Wedding Anniversary.

My daughters say of their late Mother "She was unselfish, loving, caring and compassionate. She encouraged us and always showed an interest in everything we did. In fact her entire married life was devoted to her family.

Her love of music and simple delight in her garden were a great influence in our lives. She gave us so much, that although she may not be here any more, she will remain with us always."

• • • • • •

Sadly many of my wartime contemporaries have either died or succumbed to problems arising from frailty and memory failure.

As you will understand now, I have been fortunate in making the acquaintance of ex Laghouat prisoner of war Canadian Jim Templeton's family. The photograph of Jim and family was taken just prior to his death in 1987. I welcomed Ken (his younger son) and his wife, and also their son Michael, the grandson of Gladys, Jim's widow', with his wife Jessica, to my home here in Heighington near Lincoln. Michael and Jessica are now happily living and working in London.

Modern technology has enabled quick and accurate research into history.

News came to me unexpectedly on, 23rd June 2008 from Eric Edward a gentleman entirely unknown to me, living in Gisborne, Melbourne, Australia. He is the nephew of the late Claude

Alice

*The Templeton Family,
Bruce, Jen, Ken,
Marian, Jim and
Gladys from St John's
Newfoundland*

Belcher, the friend and colleague of the late Jim Templeton in Laghouat. Eric is writing his uncle's prisoner of war story and told me Claude died in 1992 aged eighty-one. He was one of the older prisoners.

The last I heard of Ray Davies, a seaman from the cruiser Manchester and a prisoner in Laghouat, was of his retirement with his wife in Ledbury. Some time after Ray's repatriation his ship sailed from Rosyth to participate in D Day activities, (Operation Neptune to the Navy), when it was bombed by a German aircraft. The ship was seriously damaged with buckling to the port and starboard plates. Miraculously after ten days they were relieved.

I became reunited with Donald Gray, an ex Hurricane pilot and prisoner of war in Laghouat during 1941/ 1942. His last flying mission was scheduled to take him to Malta from the aircraft carrier Ark Royal then sailing in the Mediterranean. Take off from the

Singing 'Oh vive de Gaulle' with Donald Gray...

carrier's short deck presented a hazard compounded by the fact his aircraft had been loaded with spare parts destined for Malta. Fuel limitations left no reserve for emergencies. The aircraft ran out of petrol and crashed near Tunis, where Don was captured and

...and Sharing Memories

taken to Laghouat. Other aircraft failed to make the journey and shortly afterwards the Ark Royal was sunk.

Don and I met at my home here in Heighington during 2004, but sadly he died shortly afterwards in his ninety-second year.

I know now that the American Pilot, who became a prisoner of war in Laghouat and to whom I referred earlier, was Bud Walcott. His wife died when they were young and in his sadness Bud sacrificed his own life at the age of forty-two.

The RAF prisoner I mentioned having sustained sunstroke and accompanying dysentery in Laghouat was John Lewery, with whom I have been in contact recently. He was an air gunner during the war but later qualified to become a civilian pilot and bought his own aeroplane, which he still possesses. Whimsically, he tells me that having several Flying Tales published helps the State Pension! Speaking to me on 14th July 2008, he said Laghouat will always be on his mind. The disbelief that we were captive of our ex allies will never be exterminated from our thoughts.

Until recently I was unaware that 29th November 1942 was the eligibility date for my entitlement to the Air Efficiency Award (AE). After making a much belated claim, I received the medal and ribbon from the Ministry of Defence Medal Office on 25th June 2008.

AE Medal and Ribbon

BOMBER COMMAND MEMORIAL

An irony enabled me to survive the war and sixty–one years later be accorded the great honour, with veteran World War Two Bomber Command WAAF Mrs Sylvia Watts, of jointly unveiling a Memorial in Lincoln Cathedral on 27th August 2006. The words on the spotlighted Memorial Ledger Stone read – "Dedicated to the men and women of Bomber Command 1939-1945 over 55000 of whom gave their lives in defence of our liberty."

Supported by The Chapter of Lincoln Cathedral, Mr R. A. 'Scotty' Scott from Welton near Lincoln with a committee of three, pioneered the successful campaign to create the Memorial and graciously nominated Sylvia and me to carry out the unveiling. The Memorial Ledger Stone, sited in the floor of the North West Transept of the Cathedral at the entrance to the Airmen's Chapel, faces the Bomber Command stained glass window. The names of twenty-seven thousand aircrew from all over the world, who lost their lives on operational flights from airfields in Lincolnshire, are inscribed in books of remembrance, carefully safeguarded for posterity in the Chapel.

> *On 27th August 2006 a day in history had been created. The men and women of Bomber Command 1939-1945 had been remembered by the finest memorial in the world, the monument of Lincoln Cathedral.*

LANCASTER FLYPAST OVER LINCOLN CATHEDRAL BEFORE UNVEILING OF THE BOMBER COMMAND MEMORIAL 27TH AUGUST 2006

Photograph courtesy of Alan W Puncher

Photograph courtesy of E Ann Smith

UNVEILING OF BOMBER COMMAND MEMORIAL AT LINCOLN CATHEDRAL 27TH AUGUST 2006

R A 'Scotty' Scott, Mrs J Sylvia Watts & J Douglas Hudson DFC AE RAFVR

Dedicated to the men and women of
BOMBER
COMMAND
1939–1945
over 55,000 of whom gave their lives
in defence of our liberty

Photographs courtesy of E Ann Smith

BOMBER COMMAND MEMORIAL TROPHY

Photograph courtesy of E Ann Smith

In appreciation of their support at the unveiling of the Bomber Command Memorial in Lincoln Cathedral on 27th August 2006, the Bomber Command Memorial Trophy - a solid silver model Lancaster was presented to the Trent Wing Unit of the Air Training Corps in 2007 at its Headquarters at Royal Air Force Digby. The Trophy was presented by Mr R A 'Scotty' Scott the Chairman of the Bomber Command Memorial Committee, Mr J Douglas Hudson DFC AE RAFVR and Mrs J Sylvia Watts Veteran WAAF joint unveilers of the Memorial.

BOMBER COMMAND MEMORIAL
TROPHY REPLICA MODEL
HW-R ROGER – 'ROOSTER' Mark III LANCASTER ND413
100 SQUADRON WALTHAM GRIMSBY
JANUARY – JULY 1944

Photograph courtesy of Yvonne F Puncher

HW-R ROGER, emblematically marked 'ROOSTER', was a 100 SQUADRON WALTHAM, GRIMSBY based Mark III LANCASTER powered by four Merlin engines. My crew received her brand new, equipped with radar aids GEE, H2S and FISHPOND on 10th January 1944.

Our first operational flight was to BRUNSWICK four nights later and the crew accomplished a full tour of thirty sorties by 6th June 1944, on which date we supported the D DAY landings. 'ROOSTER' had completed thirty-nine operational flights, including nine flown by other crews during our periods on leave.

This was our successful crew:

Pilot	Flt Lt Jack K Hamilton DFC (Canadian)
Navigator	Fg Off J Douglas Hudson DFC RAFVR
Flight Engineer	Flt Sgt 'Billy' Bloomfield
Bomb Aimer	Fg Off Douglas H Chapman DFC
Wireless Operator/Air Gunner	Flt Sgt Dennis Lacey
Mid Upper Gunner	Flt Sgt 'Bernie' Phillips DFM
Rear Gunner	Fg Off Johnny M Hesp DFC DFM

'ROOSTER' went on to complete fifty-five operational sorties. Many of the later ones were flown by Pilot Officer D G Mills' crew, before the aircraft crashed at Irby Top, near Aylesby off the Waltham circuit on 21st July 1944 killing four of the crew as listed. Three survived although seriously injured.

Pilot	Plt Off David G Mills killed
Navigator	Flt Sgt Dick Amory killed (American)
Wireless Operator/Air Gunner	Flt Sgt Len Fisher killed
Flight Engineer	Flt Sgt Ron Crabb killed
Bomb Aimer	Flt Sgt Jack Irwin survivor
Mid Upper Gunner	Flt Sgt Bert Wells survivor
Rear Gunner	Flt Sgt Bert Fuller survivor

J DOUGLAS HUDSON DFC AE RAFVR
Navigator
101 Blenheim Squadron West Raynham
POW in Vichy French North Africa
100 Lancaster Squadron Waltham

ALICE HUDSON LRAM ARCM
His wife
Epitomised the undemonstrative bravery of
the women on the ground, who in times of
great danger, supported their heroes in the
air throughout World War Two

THE AVRO LANCASTER
As described by the Author in:
"There and Back Again" – A NAVIGATOR'S STORY
By J Douglas Hudson DFC

The Lancaster could be our salvation, our cradle or perhaps our coffin. She possessed weaponry of matchless peer. Loved or hated, her potential powers of destruction from the air were unequalled. She bolstered the morale of a British public, which had been tyrannized since 1940 by the Nazi aerial war machine, the enemy war machine, which had killed thousands of civilians and left countless thousands homeless. She bolstered the morale of an even greater European public, living under German occupation and subjected to the Nazi yoke. The roar of her engines and of her sisters' engines as they thundered overhead on their way to the German targets, gave those beleaguered citizens new hope. Now she was helping us to fight back and destroy the German infrastructure, their factories, lines of communications and all that contributed to the continuation of their war effort. Rugged, robust and reliable she remonstrated only when ill-treated. As the devil incarnate she terrorised and was feared and hated by the enemy. She obeyed our bidding.

Rocked in her cradle and in the warmth of her cabin I was able to suppress the dreaded fears of adverse possibilities. Calmed by the comforting continuous roar of her engines, which drowned all other extraneous noises, time would pass quickly for me as I worked incessantly until we reached the target. Then I would go up front, look around and take in the awesome proceedings. If we were flying in a later wave, the target would be already well alight and on nights of clear downward visibility burning buildings in the streets 20,000 feet below would be clearly discernible.

On bombing occasions, the aerial scene above most targets at around 20,000 feet was comparable with that I described over Leipzig. It was a scene we had learned to expect and to accept. As the observer, one's turn had not arrived, one felt almost detached from the horrors, yet every blazing bomber aircraft would become a 'crematorium'. Seven men entombed had to die.

Photograph from 'There & Back Again – A Navigator's Story'

THE CREW OF HW 'R' ROGER OF 100 SQUADRON RAF
WALTHAM 1944 – to become

Flt Lt J K Hamilton DFC, Flt Sgt 'Billy' Bloomfield, Fg Off J D Hudson DFC,
Fg Off D H Chapman DFC, Flt Sgt D Lacey, Flt Sgt 'Bernie' Phillips DFM,
Fg Off J M Hesp DFC DFM

Photograph courtesy of Alan W Puncher

J Douglas Hudson DFC AE RAFVR

with 'Phantom of the Ruhr' Battle of Britain Memorial Flight 27th April 2007

Lincolnshire Aviation Heritage Centre – East Kirkby
The Home of Lancaster 'Just Jane'

Photograph courtesy of E Ann Smith

In the Hangar

Photograph courtesy of Yvonne F Puncher

Returning from a taxi run

23rd of May 2009 at Lincolnshire Aviation Heritage Centre East Kirby

Douglas with Michal Juran and his colleagues from the Czech Republic

Douglas with Doreen Ainscough

Douglas with Harold and Fred Panton proprietors of the Heritage Centre

Douglas with Lancaster Bomber Veterans addressing visitors at the Heritage Centre

Douglas with Sandra Morton book signing in the hangar

27th of April 2007 at Battle of Britain Memorial Flight RAF Coningsby (unveiling of the Lancaster as 100 Squadron's Phantom of the Ruhr HW-R)

Douglas with Air Chief Marshall Sir Clive Loader

On the 26th July 2008 a special personal day in history was created for two ex Vichy French North African British prisoners of war. Ted Clayton OBE and I had not met since repatriation from Laghouat Sahara Desert prisoner of war camp on 12th November 1942. Destiny decreed we should meet again and the photograph below bears testimony to this unique and wonderful occasion, which took place at Ted's daughter and son-in-law's beautiful house and gardens in Northamptonshire.

Ted's recovery from a recent stroke has left him currently paralysed on the left side but mentally as alert as over sixty years ago, when he was 'Registrar' of Laghouat's burgeoning 'university', overseeing ninety-eight separate lecture groups.

We sang together the classic song 'Oh Vive De-Gaulle' of Aumale and Laghouat fame, which in those days kept our spirits alive and riled our Vichy French German/Italian collaborators.

The colonnades of Laghouat military caserne ceased to confine about one thousand sailors, soldiers and airmen sixty-seven years ago. The souls of many of these men later departed the cloisters of this Sahara Desert Cathedral. Unobliterated by the sands of time the cloisters continue to confine the hearts of those surviving.

'AT THE GOING DOWN OF THE SUN
AND IN THE MORNING
WE WILL REMEMBER THEM'

ACKNOWLEDGEMENTS

It was not until the year 2000 I decided to start writing my wartime memoirs. Fifty-five to sixty years later may seem a long time before recording this chapter in my life's history. Motivation arrived from an unexpected source, from two very dedicated people, who were previously unknown to me. I am indebted to my bomb-aimer Douglas Chapman who was responsible for our introduction.

Nick and Carol Carter had devoted a great deal of their time in detailed research to compile and publish a register of all recipients of The Distinguished Flying Cross 1918-1995. Two copies of this register they kindly donated to the Royal Air Force Benevolent Fund to be auctioned to raise funds for this cause.

I was delighted, a little later, to welcome them to our home and it was during this visit they suggested that if I were to chronicle my wartime experiences, they might be of interest to others.

Thank you Nick and Carol.

I also acknowledge the help of my immediate family and thank them for their patience, co-operation and advice; also my son-in-law Alan, whose expertise on computer and scanner was responsible initially for the upgrading and reproduction of photographs.

• • • • • •

DURING MY NAVIGATIONAL JOURNEY I MET MANY PEOPLE OF FASCINATING AND DIFFERENT PERSUASIONS. WITHOUT THE HELPFUL INFLUENCE OF THE UNDERMENTIONED, MY MEMOIRS COULD NOT HAVE BEEN COMPLETED.

Flight Lieutenant Dawson	Manchester RAFVR
Sergeant Harry Bowers	Manchester RAFVR
Sergeant Ted Hart	North Africa
Flight Sergeant Stevens DFM BEM	North Africa
Sergeant John Riddick	
101 Squadron West Raynham and North Africa	
Sergeant 'Tony' D.W.G. Randall	
	101 Squadron West Raynham and North Africa
French Lieutenant (Name unknown)	North Africa
Flight Lieutenant 'Cap' Cooper	North Africa
Private 'Daffy' Watson	North Africa
Corporal Ted Clayton	North Africa
Flight Lieutenant 'Bertie' Brain DFC	North Africa
Lieutenant Commander Watkins	North Africa
Sergeant 'Wilbur' Wright	North Africa
Commander R.F. Jessel DSO	North Africa
Pilot Officer J.M. Alexander	North Africa
Captain Montgomery	North Africa
Squadron Leader Brickell	North Africa
Sergeant Claude Belcher NZ	North Africa
Commandant Jeunechamp	Laghouat
Eight Premier Spahis Cavalry Soldiers	Laghouat
Sergeant 'Digger' Aubrey Latter Australian	North Africa
Sergeant H.C. Gibbins	North Africa
Flight Lieutenant J.K. Hamilton DFC	Wymeswold
	100 Squadron Waltham
Sergeant W.F. Bloomfield	Wymeswold
	100 Squadron Waltham
Flying Officer D.H. Chapman DFC	Wymeswold
	100 Squadron Waltham
Flight Sergeant 'Sparks' Denis F.H. Lacey	Wymeswold
	100 Squadron Waltham

Pilot Officer 'Jack' I.J. Duffett   Wymeswold
           100 Squadron Waltham

Squadron Leader L.C. Pipkin DFC & Bar   Wymeswold

Pilot Officer J.M. Hesp DFC DFM   100 Squadron Waltham

Sergeant B.R. Phillips DFM   100 Squadron Waltham

Flight Lieutenant G.R. Ross   100 Squadron Waltham

Flying Officer Beck   100 Squadron Waltham

Wing Commander R.V.L. Pattison DSO DFC
100 Squadron Waltham

Squadron Leader H.H. Grant Dalton DFC & Bar
100 Squadron Waltham

Pilot Officer T.F. Cook DFC   100 Squadron Waltham

Flight Lieutenant Eric W. Norman DFC   100 Squadron Waltham

Squadron Leader 'Doc' Marshall   100 Squadron Waltham and
      Sandtoft Station Medical Officer

The ranks and awards of the services' personnel are, as I knew them.

· · · · · ·

Air Chief Marshal Sir Clive Loader KCB OBE ADC FRAeS RAF
      Commander-in-Chief Air Command

The Very Reverend Dr Alec Knight
      former Dean of Lincoln Cathedral

Canon Gavin Kirk   Precentor of Lincoln

Canon Alan Nugent   Subdean of Lincoln Cathedral

Mr Roy Bentham   Chapter Clerk and Chief Executive
      Lincoln Cathedral

Mr Michael Morris   Sculptor - Lincoln Cathedral

Mr R.A. 'Scotty' Scott Flight Lieutenant RAF Retired
      Chairman Bomber Command Memorial Committee

Squadron Leader Alastair Scott
      Bomber Command Memorial Committee

Mr Roy Fleckney Warrant Officer RAF Retired
      Bomber Command Memorial Committee

Mr Eric Moss-Wright   Accountant & Advisor to
      Bomber Command Memorial Committee

Mrs J. Sylvia Watts   Veteran Bomber Command WAAF

Mrs Dawn Bowskill   Welton Lincoln

Mr Ben Hudston   Welton Lincoln
Wing Commander David Speed MBE RAFVR (T)
            Officer Commanding Trent Wing Air Training Corps
Squadron Leader David Hortop BA (Hons) RAFVR (T)
                  Air Training Corps Trent Wing & Cadets
Miss Sandra Morton M.Sc. MBA FIBMS CSci.
Doreen Ainscough   Writer/historian West Yorkshire
Mr Bruce Smith   Edinburgh
Mr Kenneth A. Templeton Q.C.   St. John's, Newfoundland
Mr Fred Panton MBE   The Lincolnshire Aviation
Mr Harold Panton   Heritage Centre
The Panton Families   East Kirkby

Squadron Leader Al Pinner MBE former Officer Commanding and all members of the Battle of Britain Memorial Flight RAF Coningsby, the Visitors' Centre and all other dedicated staff.

MARGARET IDE

Daughter of Billy Ide Sussex County Cricketer, Margaret Ide a veteran WW2 WAAF radar operator, died suddenly aged eighty-eight on 31st March 2009. She married during WW2 and our families became associated in Warwickshire during 1954. Her daughters played with our daughters enjoying the mysteries of our beautiful Highclere garden as depicted on pages 184/186. The girls, with whom my families are in regular contact, grew up together and now have their own families. Margaret was a friend and for many years a voluntary social worker with my late wife. She will be greatly missed.

Key to Photographs of Personnel Whose Names I Recall

Page 36
Le Kef Winter 1940/41

Back Row
1. Eric Shipley (Camp Echo Artist) 2. French Guard
3. Plt Off Ferguson 4. Bill Stevens 5. Fg Off Dai Davies 6. John Riddick
7. 'Cap' Cooper 8. French Guard 9. Tony Randall 10. Plt Off Smith NZ
Centre Row
1. Jock Burnett 2. French Guard 3. French Official
Front Row
1. Self 2. Wilbur Wright 3. French Guard 4. Ted Hart 5. French Guard

Page 86
Mark 1 Latrine Laghouat

Back Row
3. Barney Todd 5. Sqn Ldr Brickell 6. Self 10. Jim Templeton
One on his own
Bill Stevens
Third Row
1. Wilcox
Second Row
4. Plt Off Ferguson 5. Ted Hart 8. (standing) H.C. Gibbins
Front Row
4. Wilbur Wright 5. 'Digger' Latter 7. Mick Steer

Page 103
Back Row
1. Bob Turner 9. Jimmy Alexander 10. Tony Randall
Centre Row
1. Wilcox 2. Ted Clayton 8. Daffy Watson
Front Row
1. American pilot (see page 139) 3. Self

Page 110
Group Photograph Laghouat December 1941
Back Row
1. Macdonald?
Second Row
1. Bill Ballard 2. Sqn Ldr Brickell 5. (crouching) French Guard
6. 'Digger' Latter
Front Row
2. Pickles 5. Mick Cook? 6. 'Cap' Cooper 7. Mick Steer

Page 119
'AMENITY slit trench'

1. Sgt Macdonald 3. Plt Off Smith 4. Captain Montgomery 5. Lt Robairre

"Whilst a war baby exercising my lungs during the later stages of World War Two, young men and women were volunteering for service with the Royal Air Force.

I later learned to read of the many sacrificial exploits of the personnel of Bomber Command and they became my heroes. With over 55,000 men and women killed, their part in the war effort was of the greatest magnitude.

Later, when teaching history from the immediate past, I used family veterans and artefacts to give children a complete hands-on history education. I determined that Bomber Command history would be faithfully retold.

According to the comments of Winston Churchill the fighters were our salvation, but the bombers alone provided the means of victory.

Sadly, no official Bomber Command medal in recognition has ever been forthcoming.

Those alive, with their continuing modesty, still deserve my total respect and gratitude, as does the remembrance of those who died with life stretching before them

They are my heroes still."

Doreen Ainscough

"To those who gave their all

Remembering Douglas Hudson DFC RAFVR and his many thousands of comrades of RAF Bomber Command 1939 - 1945.

These men flew into hell and back, time after time and played a major part in destroying the evil Nazi war machine.

Also remembering the thousands of dedicated RAF women and men who toiled day and night with great skill and determination to keep the aircraft flying.

As a schoolboy, I was witness to much of the air activity in Lincolnshire and I watched in awe and great admiration.

I can never thank these heroes enough for giving me and millions of people like me, the right to live in peace and freedom.

We must never forget them."

Stanley Baldwin - Lincolnshire

JUSTIFICATION

To help preserve liberty it is known that during World War Two 1939-1945, nearly 56,000 men and women of Bomber Command, mostly aircrew from all over the world, gave their lives without counting the cost.

These photos of the grandchildren of my niece Judy Lyn Park and her devoted husband, tell an important story. Jenny and Samuel are ambassadorial of the countless thousands of children born after the end of The Second World War in countries free of Nazi German occupation.

The sacrifices that enabled this emancipation, for which we give our thanks to God, were not made in vain.

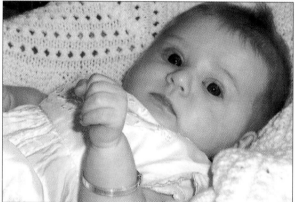

Jenny

Samuel

Sandra my neighbour, supportive friend and lady of positive thinking

(Photograph taken at Lincoln Cathedral after unveiling of The Bomber Command Memorial Ledger Stone on 27th August 2006)

My granddaughter Emma and grandson David, brother of Andrew, the priceless legacies of my daughters Ann and Yvonne respectively (Photograph taken at Lincoln Cathedral after unveiling of The Bomber Command Memorial Ledger Stone on 27th August 2006)

My grandson Andrew with his wife Charlotte

Douglas with elder daughter Ann (left) and Yvonne in Lincoln Cathedral after unveiling of the Bomber Command Memorial Ledger Stone on 27th August 2006

Optimism is eternal without which life is naught
Polaris is the navigator's Shepherd
The Lord is my Shepherd
WORLD WITHOUT END